DIVINE

DISCIPLINES

*God's Training Ground for
Spiritual Growth and Maturity*

Bobby Mullins

innovo
PUBLISHING

Published by Innovo Publishing, LLC
www.innovopublishing.com
1-888-546-2111

innovo
P U B L I S H I N G

Providing Full-Service Publishing Services for
Christian Authors, Artists & Organizations: Hardbacks, Paperbacks, eBooks,
Audiobooks, Music & Videos

DIVINE DISCIPLINES:
God's Training Ground for Spiritual Growth and Maturity

Library of Congress Control Number: 2017953302
ISBN: 978-1-61314-404-6

Cover Design & Interior Layout: Innovo Publishing, LLC

Printed in the United States of America
U.S. Printing History
First Edition: October 2017

DEDICATION

Dedicated to my earthly parents, Raymond and Vadine Mulllins, who were examples in human form of how we are disciplined by God, as a parent to a child, for our best.

CONTENTS

PREFACE

There is no development of Christ-likeness in a person's life apart from suffering. Christians are not exempt from experiencing trials, problems, and suffering. Difficulties are necessary occurrences in the growth and development of our Christian lives. As a matter of fact, God not only allows adversity, but he even brings it upon us, at times. He does not do so because we lack faith or because of our spiritual disobedience, but he also uses adversity to increase our faith. Trials, testings, and tribulation help us to grow and mature into the people of faith whom God wants us to be.

This book is going to examine a topic that has had little written about it, although it is something that all Christians experience. Many Christians are living in a state of defeat, depression, discontent, and discouragement because they do not have a knowledge or proper understanding of divine discipline from God. It yields wonderful benefits in the lives of those "who have been trained by it" (Heb. 12:11).

An awareness and understanding of divine discipline will spiritually revive, renew, and refresh the lives of Christians who are not living daily in the joy of the Lord. It will take spiritually mature, growing Christians to a higher level of faith. In coming to a fuller knowledge and proper understanding of divine discipline, I have been spiritually enlightened and emotionally encouraged and relieved. I now see that what I had looked back upon as painful and hurtful experiences of my past, oftentimes were actually situations carefully orchestrated under the providential direction of God, who was working in those circumstances according to the counsel and purpose of his will for my life (Eph. 1:11) and for my good (Rom. 8:28).

Hebrews 12:4-11 will be the source Bible text for this book and its subject of divine discipline. In this passage, the writer of Hebrews discusses the *purpose*, *practice*, and *product* of God's divine discipline of Christians. The text specifically reveals the purpose for which Christians are disciplined and the product (end result) of that discipline. The practice (the manner by which God disciplines us) of divine discipline is not revealed in this passage, but examples of divine discipline are illustrated elsewhere in the scriptures, and some of those examples will be examined in this book.

In the text in chapter twelve of Hebrews, the Greek word, *paideia*, is used eight times. There are two ways the most popular English Bible versions translate this Greek word into English, either as "discipline" or "chastening." The Living Bible paraphrase uses "punish" or "correction." I prefer the translation, "discipline," for *paideia* in the Hebrews 12. When taking into account all that the writer of Hebrews has said prior to Hebrews 12:4-11, the context of these verses does not support an exclusive translation of *paideia* that only gives a picture in English of being punished, disciplined, or chastened because one has disobeyed God by sinning intentionally or unintentionally. The suffering and persecution, which the original readers of Hebrews were experiencing, would come because of their being obedient to God. In this passage, God has revealed that he allows suffering, persecution, and chastening to discipline us to maturity in our Christian faith.

Now God does cause us to suffer as a way of punishing us for disobedience, but all our discipline from God is not because we have done something wrong. God uses difficulties and hardships as a means of needed correction, but they are also God's methods of helpful, faith-maturing discipline. *Divine discipline is the training ground for spiritual growth and maturity.*

1: The Purpose of Divine Discipline

"For Our Best"

You have not yet resisted to bloodshed, striving against sin. And you have forgotten the exhortation which speaks to you as to sons: "My son, do not despise the chastening of the LORD, Nor be discouraged when you are rebuked by Him; For whom the LORD loves He chastens, And scourges every son whom He receives." If you endure chastening, God deals with you as with sons; for what son is there whom a father does not chasten? But if you are without chastening, of which all have become partakers, then you are illegitimate and not sons.

Furthermore, we have had human fathers who corrected us, and we paid them respect. Shall we not much more readily be in subjection to the Father of spirits and live? For they indeed for a few days chastened us as seemed best to them, but He for our profit, that we may be partakers of His holiness. Now no chastening seems to be joyful for the present, but painful; nevertheless, afterward it yields the peaceable fruit of righteousness to those who have been trained by it. (Heb. 12:4-11)

Before disciplining you because of misbehavior, perhaps one of your parents actually expressed to you the well-known cliche, "This is going to hurt me more than it is going to hurt you." Of course, you never believed it! As a father who felt it necessary, at times, to discipline my children, I do understand the intent of that much-used statement. The emotional hurt I felt was not as physically painful as that of my children, but I hurt too, especially when my children got so repentant before they were disciplined.

Why did I discipline my children for misbehavior if it hurt me as well as them? Well, it is biblical. God tells us in his Word that it is necessary in order to properly train our children (Prov. 13:24; 22:15; 23:13-14; 29:15, 17). I also disciplined my children because I believed it was for their good. It was certainly not pleasurable, but the Bible teaches that it is best when our children receive correction for improper displays of behavior. But I also disciplined my children in positive ways, as they grew older. It was not because of something they did wrong, but it was to teach and train them in what is necessary to exist in life. For instance, we discipline our children to learn how to dress themselves, to feed themselves, to read and write, to carry on a proper conservation, to develop balanced work and play habits, and to get proper rest.

God disciplines his children in like manner. Actually, *we* discipline our children in the manner and means by which *God* disciplines us. Hebrews 12:10 emphasizes that as earthly fathers discipline their children as seems best to them, God disciplines us *for our best*. The discipline of God is for our best because it is to our advantage and for our profit.

In Hebrews 12:4-11, four reasons are given for the divine discipline of God and why it is for our best. It is for the purpose of *conforming* us, *confirming* us, *correcting* us, and *resting* us. In the first three verses of Hebrews 12, the writer had called on the readers to lay aside their sins, which hindered a victorious Christian life. As a runner removes warm-up garments that could slow him down as he is about to run a race, Christians need to deal with the sin in our lives that hinder our growth and witness for Christ. The writer of Hebrews next revealed that the way to overcome the sins that weigh us down, and the way to keep us enduring in the race of life, is in keeping our focus on Jesus and reflecting upon the suffering Christ endured for us as the author and finisher of our faith.

Beginning in verse four, the writer reminded the readers of Hebrews that unlike Christ, they had not been persecuted to the point of death on account of their Christian faith. He then reminded them in verse five, quoting from Proverbs 3:11, to not take lightly the discipline of the Lord and to not become despondent or discouraged when

10

corrected or reproved by the Lord. In this verse, the writer was referring to discipline resulting from wrongdoing or disobedience to God. But the overall emphasis of the writer in this passage is that whatever the reason for which God may discipline us, we are not to lose courage, get despondent, get "down in the dumps," or retreat. The divine discipline of God is for our best.

Conforming Us

A purpose of the divine discipline of God is for *conforming* us. Verses four and five of Hebrews 12 say, "You have not yet resisted to bloodshed, striving against sin. And you have forgotten the exhortation which speaks to you as to sons: 'My son, do not despise the chastening of the LORD, Nor be discouraged when you are rebuked by Him.'" The specific way by which God wants to conform us, in light of these two verses, is by building courage in our lives.

In verses two and three, the writer reminded the readers how Christ did not give up, and neither should they give up. As Jesus stood firm in his commitment to endure suffering in order to fulfill the will of his Father, the writer was trying to build courage in the readers of Hebrews by encouraging them that they, too, could endure suffering in fulfilling the will of God. At those times, when they were tempted to become weary and discouraged, they were to consider the suffering Christ had endured for them at Calvary. If they would respond obediently to the discipline of God, then they would have the courage to endure suffering, even unto death, to fulfill their heavenly Father's will.

Three basic ways were revealed by which courage was to be built into the lives of the original readers of Hebrews, and they are applicable for our lives today. First, the building of courage begins with *obedience to God's Word*. The readers of Hebrews were not to forget the exhortation to them from the Word of God. After the writer of Hebrews made that statement, he then quoted from the book of Proverbs. Earlier in the letter, the readers were exhorted to "give the more earnest heed" to the things which they had heard, lest they would "drift away" (Heb. 2:1). That statement was made after several verses were quoted from the book of Psalms. The reminder to the readers was for them to remember and take seriously what God said. The writer took the Word of God seriously, as he quoted from it to get his point across.

If you keep in the Word, it will keep you from the snares of the world. But all who hear the truth of God's Word will not heed it. When that is the case, such a person is likely to drift away from its teachings. Their faith will become weaker instead of stronger. Courage will not be built into their life, and they will not be conformed to the will of God. So we are to be responsible to act upon that which we hear from the Word of God.

A second basic way we are conformed to the will of God is by *not overlooking God's discipline*. The writer said, "Do not despise the chastening of the Lord" (Heb. 12:5). We are not to be indifferent to the discipline of God. God works through the adversities of life just as he works through the pleasant experiences. But many Christians are unaware or apathetic of this fact. It may be that God has put you in difficult circumstances to get you to the point of hearing something he wants to say to you. While everything seems to be going well in your life, you are not paying attention to what God is trying to say to you.

> *There are times when God may have to reduce you to nothing so that he becomes your everything in order that he can do anything he wants to do through you.*

At an evangelism conference in 1986, I heard the late Jerry Falwell say that if he had two good days back to back, his prayer life suffered. He explained that when things are always going our way, we tend to get self-sufficient, and we do not lean on God and follow his guidance as we should. So the Lord sends adversity our way to keep us leaning on him. There are times when God may have to reduce you to nothing so that he becomes your everything in order that he can do anything he wants to do through you. Our adversities may be to renew our commitment of our entire life to the Lord. They may be for the purpose of reviving convictions that are the same as his convictions so that we desire to do God's will above all else. His sending adversity could be for restoring our confidence in his ability to completely provide for and care for us. Specifically, in

Hebrews 12:4-5, we learn that God disciplines us through adversity to build courage in our lives that will reflect conformity to Christ, whatever the circumstances may be. Those are only a few examples of why God allows or brings adversity upon us. If God is disciplining you in such a manner, do not overlook it. Be aware of and alert to the means he has chosen to conform you to his will.

A third way the divine discipline of God conforms us to Christ-likeness is by our *not being overwhelmed by adversity*. Do not "be discouraged when you are rebuked by Him" (Heb. 12:5). We are not to lose courage when God brings hardships upon us. One reason why God does not want us to be overwhelmed by adversity is that we might be a witness in the storms of life. Our staying steady, consistent, and true to the Lord in our troubles can be a witness to the unsaved and an encouragement to other Christians who are experiencing difficulties (1 Pet. 5:9). God conforms us to the likeness of his Son (Rom. 8:29) so that our lifestyle witness will draw and lead others to follow Christ.

Life is going to see its adversities. Jesus said, "In the world you will have tribulation" (John 16:33). But just prior to that statement the Lord said, "In me you might have peace." The verse concludes with Christ's encouragement to "be of good cheer, I have overcome the world." We do not need to be overwhelmed by trials, troubles, and tribulation because of our way through the storms of life. It is through Jesus that we have peace in the midst of the storms, and we overcome them by keeping our focus and attention on Christ (Heb. 12:1-2). Just remember, the Lord who disciplines us is also the Lord who delivers us.

Confirming Us

A second purpose for the divine discipline of God is to *confirm* us. Because of his compassion, we are disciplined by God for our proof, our profit, and as our privilege.

The divine discipline of God is *a confirmation of proof* that we belong to the family of God. His discipline verifies that we are his children. The Bible says that "whom the Lord loves He chastens, and scourges every son whom He receives" (Heb. 12:6). The Lord disciplines those whom he loves as an earthly father deals with his children (Heb. 12:7).

It validates his compassion for us. Who loves more? Is it the father who allows his child to do whatever he wants to do, even if it is harmful? Or, does the father love more who corrects, trains, and, when necessary, punishes his child to help him learn what is right? The discipline of a father shows proof of his love for his child. The divine discipline of God is proof that confirms you are one of his children.

Divine discipline is also *a cause of profit* for us because it matures us in our faith. The discipline of a father is for our best and for our profit (Heb. 12:10) when he does it out of love. Because of his compassion and care, a father disciplines his child. When a child realizes his father disciplines him out of love, for his profit, it brings the child into a far deeper relationship with his father.

Divine discipline is also of profit to us because it distends the range of our faith. This one word, *distend*, is not used often in our everyday language, but it is the word that best illustrates what divine discipline does for our faith. Distend means to become larger, to expand, and to stretch out in all directions. Divine discipline brings us into a far deeper experience in the level of faith we have reached in our pilgrimage as followers of Christ. As we allow it to train us (Heb. 12:11), our faith is deepened, heightened, widened, and continuously stretched out in all directions, far beyond what we ever imagined possible.

As members of the family of God, we not only receive certain privileges and security, but adversity also comes with it. The apostle Paul said of the Christian life, "For to you it has been granted on behalf of Christ, not only to believe in Him, but also to suffer for His sake" (Phil. 1:29). Divine discipline, in the form of adversity, is *a claim of privilege* for the Christian. You should expect it. The writer of Hebrews said, "But if you are without chastening, of which all have become partakers, then you are illegitimate and not sons" (Heb. 12:8). Adversity may come upon you for chastening, correction, guidance, or direction, but it confirms you are one of God's children.

Not only should you expect firm discipline from the Lord, even in the form of suffering, but you must learn to respect it. Hebrews 12:9 says, "Furthermore, we have had human fathers who corrected us, and we paid them respect. Shall we not much more readily be in subjection to the Father of spirits and live?" As a father who really loves his children is

14

concerned that they should realize their potential and grow to maturity, God desires the same for his children. Without discipline, children will remain immature, childish, and undeveloped. Knowing God is disciplining us, because it is for our best, is worthy of our respect. Divine discipline confirms our relationship as privileged members of his family.

Correcting Us

A third purpose for the divine discipline of God is for *correcting* us. His correcting us is to keep us rightly related to him. We need to have the right attitude in how we respond to his discipline. A Christian should *accept God's discipline* in a spirit of submission because of the assurance we have been given that it is for our best. As we are submissive to divine discipline, it is then that we really begin to live, according to the writer of Hebrews. To exhibit the right attitude in accepting divine discipline, self-control will be necessary, especially when adversity is part of the discipline. Strive to remain positive in the midst of divine discipline by looking for the life lesson God wants you to learn or, in some cases, to unlearn. Focus your mind on the truth that as our earthly fathers chastened us as seemed best to them, God also does so for our profit, that we may be partakers of his holiness (Heb. 12:10).

It is important that we also *approve God's discipline*. We often will accept the way something is but not necessarily like it. For instance, we may say that we accept our present situation in life. Yet we often find ourselves complaining about our job, our salary, or our home, to the point that we are envious of things others have that we do not have. If that is the case, we have not really accepted the present situation God has allowed us to be in. When you approve your lot in life, then you are agreeing with the Lord concerning his will for your life. God can reverse your situation anytime he desires, but he wants you at a place of submissiveness where he can "will and do for His good pleasure" (Phil. 2:13) with you.

It has been emphasized several times in this chapter that the divine discipline of God is for our best. When God is doing something for our best, even when it is difficult, we can be thankful by considering "that all things work together for good to those who love God, to those who are the called according to His purpose" (Rom. 8:28). If you are seeking to live for God, then he will work all things for your best. For some, this life may see one trial after another, but that is how the purpose of God is fulfilled in their witness for Christ (see Heb. 11:8-40). Later in this book, we will study the divine discipline of differences. There are divine differences in position, persecution, and personality. You may feel that you are on the down side of divine differences, but you can still find a reason to rejoice, even when you feel that someone else is getting a better break in life. The passage in Romans 8, concluding with verse 28, begins in verse 18, stating, "For I consider that the sufferings of this present time are not worthy to be compared with the glory which shall be revealed in us." The glory mentioned in that verse is the inherent future glory in us which we will experience in heaven.

We can learn to approve God's discipline because we know he is working for our good while we are pilgrims on this earth, moving toward our eternal home in heaven. We have been promised, too, that nothing on this earth can ever separate us from the love of God through Christ (Rom. 8:35-39), a love so great that it led Jesus to die for our sins so that we might have eternal life in heaven through our faith, belief, and trust in Christ. We have been separated and set apart by God for Christ. His will may include "tribulation, distress, persecution, or famine." But we are never separated from the love of God, although we may be separated from the comforts of life.

Many people today have it all materially, yet they are not satisfied and happy. When I am obediently doing what the Lord wants me to do, regardless of where I am, that is when I know satisfaction. It satisfies me! Satisfied is a wonderful place to be.

In realizing that divine discipline is for your best, it makes it easier to *appreciate God's discipline*. Although divine discipline can be very difficult, at times, part of its purpose is to bring you happiness. Happiness is an emotion that, for the most part, is dependent on outward circumstances. But you can learn to be happy, even when outward circumstances are not always what you would like them to be. The Bible says, "A merry heart makes a cheerful countenance, . . . But he who is of a merry heart has a continual feast" (Prov. 15:13, 15). God may have you in a period of difficulty so that your remaining merry and cheerful will be an encouragement and witness to others who are experiencing the same difficulty. Isn't it a happy thought that God thinks so highly of you that he can bring difficulty on you to help others?

Another motivation to help us appreciate God's discipline is that it can make you a healthier person. Normally, a happy person is physically a healthier person. Proverbs 17:22 reminds us that "a merry heart does good, like medicine." From the third chapter of Proverbs, a chapter from which the writer of Hebrews quotes in Hebrews 12:5-6, the Bible says that responding positively to God's commands and to his correction will bring "length of days," "long life," "peace," "health to your flesh," and "strength to your bones" (Prov. 3:1-2, 7-8). Now there are cases where an obedient, committed Christian experiences poor health or is physically handicapped, but those individuals are often healthier in spirit than those who are in better physical health. If a godly, appreciative spirit and attitude does not add years to one's life, it will definitely add life to one's years.

> *God's discipline and correction is not meant to bring heaviness or hurtfulness, but it is meant to produce happiness and healthiness, if we allow it to exercise us for the intended purpose of God.*

God's discipline and correction is not meant to bring heaviness or hurtfulness, but it is meant to produce happiness and healthiness, if we allow it to exercise us for the intended purpose of God. However, even though divine discipline results in happiness and healthiness, that is not God's ultimate purpose for it, especially in correcting us. The ultimate purpose of God in his correction and discipline is "that we may be partakers of His holiness" (Heb. 12:10). Oswald Chambers said,

> The destined end of man is not happiness, nor health, but holiness. . . . God has one destined end for mankind, holiness. His one aim is the production of saints. God is not an eternal blessing machine for men; . . . Never tolerate through sympathy with yourself or with others any practice that is not in keeping with a holy God. Holiness means unsullied walking with the feet, unsullied talking with the tongue, unsullied thinking with the mind—every detail of life under

the scrutiny of God. Holiness is not only what God gives me, but what I manifest that God has given me."[1]

God says that "you shall be holy, for I am holy" (Lev. 11:44). The Bible says, "The LORD will establish you as a holy people to Himself, just as He has sworn to you, if you keep the commandments of the LORD your God and walk in His ways" (Deut. 28:9). As we have had human fathers who corrected us (Heb. 12:9) when we disobeyed them, God also disciplines us to correct our disobedience to his commands and his ways. The ultimate purpose of the divine discipline of God in correcting us is that we may become holy as he is holy. As his children, our desire should be to become as much like our Father, our Creator, who loves us with an everlasting love (Jer. 31:3). We should make it a goal that our natural response to divine discipline is to accept, approve, and appreciate it.

RESTING US

There is a fourth purpose given in Hebrews 12 for the divine discipline of God. It is given in verse 11: "Now no chastening seems to be joyful for the present, but painful; nevertheless, afterward it yields the peaceable fruit of righteousness to those who have been trained by it." Divine discipline is not only for the purpose of conforming, confirming, and correcting us, but it is also for *resting* us.

Contentment is satisfaction with whatever your circumstances are in life (Phil. 4:11), when you know that you are striving to do what God wants you to do. Adversity goes against the core of our human intellect and emotions. When we are being disciplined, it does not seem to be joyful at the time. But if we allow it to exercise us and train us, the result is *contentment*. To be trained to a state of contentment by divine discipline brings a lifestyle of patience and a positive outlook on life.

Patience is accepting everything that happens to me as being from God or allowed by God, without giving him a deadline to remove it and without wavering in faith. Not being a patient person is a sin that many Christians try to explain away. Too often I have even heard preachers

1.   Oswald Chambers, *My Utmost for His Highest*, (Burlington, Ontario, Canada: Welch Publishing Company, Inc. by permission of Dodd, Mead and Company, 1963), 180.

admit, in a braggadocios manner, that they are not patient when it comes to "doing the Lord's work." They almost make it appear that the Lord does not frown on impatience. They try to justify their impatience with the excuse, "The Lord's work can't wait. It must be done right now." But even when it comes to accomplishing some of the things we feel led to do as part of the work of the Lord, he tells us in his Word to be patient. Luke 8:15, Romans 12:12, 1 Thessalonians 1:3 and 5:14, 1 Timothy 6:11, and James 1:3-4 are just a few examples of what the Bible says about patience.

Whenever someone is impatient, and he gets one or two steps ahead of the Lord in his will and in his work, it will eventually knock the impatient person three or four steps backward. And it usually results in others being pushed back in the process too. So much of the conflict, discord, and tight financial situations in churches today is because of impatience on the part of the pastor and leaders in those churches. Patience is one of the character qualities divine discipline is meant to develop in our lives.

Patience, like satisfaction, is a wonderful state to have attained. It brings a pleasantness to life that is not dependent on comforts and conveniences. Such a person has a positive outlook on life and is enjoyable to be around. So much of what the world seeks after for contentment and satisfaction results in discontent and does not bring peace, rest, and calmness. Instead, it bears conflict, stress, and disturbance.

As divine discipline rests you by teaching you to learn to be content, it also develops consistency in your life. Content people are consistent people. As they have accepted their present lot in life, they just go about their normal duties day by day, in a cooperative, Christian spirit. Consistency is built into our lives through divine discipline. As you are trained by God's discipline, you become consistent in your persistence. You become thorough, steady, and smooth in all you do. You are not rattled or distracted by irritations and stumbling blocks that can throw a kink in your plans. Your persistence to stay at the task at hand, as you are seeking to do the will of God, results in greater effectiveness as a witness for the Lord.

Perseverance also becomes evident in your life. A popular cliché in athletic training is that "pain is gain." To be the best you can be in most anything requires discipline, and pain is part of it. The athlete in training knows this. The world record holders, particularly, in track and swimming events, go through a lot of pain to make it look so smooth and easy.

I am a jogger. It is my favorite way to exercise. I have found that for the amount of time I have for exercise, jogging is what I enjoy doing the most that provides me with the best physical benefits. I jog along at a slow, but constant and consistent pace. As I occasionally increase my amount of running and distance, I usually develop shin splints. They are painful! They make the lower part of my legs feel like one big bruise. I read an article a few years ago how one runner coped with the pain of training when he was striving for more distance at a faster speed. He said that he ran through the pain. That is what I have learned to do too. I run through the pain. As my shins adjust to the greater demand on them, eventually I can jog that longer distance and longer time without the pain of shin splints.

God will train you along the line of quality that he wants to add to your life. Most of the time it is painful, but the result is that you move to a higher level in your faith where you can face great adversity, without anxiety, without falling apart, and with a Christ-like spirit. That is when you have attained the "peaceable fruit of righteousness" (Heb. 12:11).

Hebrews 12:11 is a picture of rest. The peaceable fruit of righteousness that comes from divine discipline, if you have been trained by it, brings a calmness to your life. I have never visited Lake Placid, New York, the location of the 1980 Winter Olympics. But I like its name and the picture that comes to my mind when I hear it. God desires for his children to spiritually live around "Lake Placid." After an athlete has endured a hard practice or race, he rests.

> *God will train you along the line of quality that he wants to add to your life.*

God wants to see us in a state of rest between his times of divine discipline, free from anxiety and fear. Although storms and difficult days will still come to our spiritual Lake Placid, the result of our training is that we will not be anxious or fearful in the midst of life's storms because we know that God will protect us, direct us, and provide for us. The more God exercises us the better trained we become. We are ready to face the next race on our life's journey, to jump over the next hurdle, and to swim through troubled waters. We know by experience that God is working for our best, that he will see us through, and that a peaceful, resting time of calm will soon come.

Conclusion

As you cooperate with God's divine discipline and are trained by it, it yields the peaceable fruit of righteousness in your life. You are not only saved from the curse of sin, through Christ (2 Cor. 5:21), but your lifestyle shows that the cure for sin, made possible by Jesus, makes a difference for the best in your life right now. Others see the peaceable fruit of righteousness in you, and they will desire to have it in their lives too.

The purpose of divine discipline is to conform us to the will of God, to confirm us as his children, to correct us where we are not holy as he is holy, and to rest us, so that we will be calm, content, consistent, and at peace in any situation, as we are obedient to abide in his will for our lives.

2: Divine Darkness

"Training Us to Hear God"

Divine Darkness: A state in which God places one in a period of extended, mostly private meditation for the purpose of producing deeper fellowship with God in order to reveal the powerful spiritual insights gleaned during this time.

There was a man in the land of Uz, whose name was Job; and that man was blameless and upright, and one who feared God and shunned evil. (Job 1:1)

Job was a man who was blameless, upright, God-fearing, and an avoider of evil. He had a high, moral character, and he lived what he professed. He was a man of integrity, fairness, and loyalty. Job had a holy, reverent respect for God. He avoided evil, and he deliberately turned from it when confronted by it. Job wanted no part of anything that was against God.

The Bible says that Job was the greatest of all the people of the East (Job 1:3). He had a wealth of possessions and property. He had seven sons and three daughters (Job 1:2). His concern for their spiritual welfare was so great that he would often rise early in the morning to intercede before God in their behalf (Job 1:5). Their family enjoyed being together (Job 1:4). Job was blessed with fame, fortune, a fine family, and a fervent faith in God.

Now there was a day when the sons of God came to present themselves before the LORD, and Satan also came among them.

And the LORD said to Satan, "From where do you come?" So Satan answered the LORD and said, "From going to and fro on the earth, and from walking back and forth on it." Then the LORD said to Satan, "Have you considered My servant Job, that there is none like him on the earth, a blameless and upright man, one who fears God and shuns evil?" So Satan answered the LORD and said, "Does Job fear God for nothing? Have You not made a hedge around him, around his household, and around all that he has on every side? You have blessed the work of his hands, and his possessions have increased in the land. But now, stretch out Your hand and touch all that he has, and he will surely curse You to Your face!" And the LORD said to Satan, "Behold, all that he has is in your power; only do not lay a hand on his person." So Satan went out from the presence of the LORD. (Job 1:6-12)

Job had it all! Yet in one day, he lost it all. The first chapter of Job records that in one day all of Job's oxen, donkeys, sheep, and camels were either destroyed or stolen. According to the text, it appeared that all but four of his servants were killed. As his sons and daughters were feasting in their oldest brother's house, a great wind caused it to fall in, and all of Job's children were crushed to death. Those tragedies occurred because God allowed them to happen. It was not because of wrongdoing on the part of Job. His simple response to this first set of tragic circumstances was, "The LORD gave, and the LORD has taken away; Blessed be the name of the LORD" (Job 1:21).

It got even worse for Job. At a later time, the Lord called again the life of Job to the attention of Satan. This second time that God asked Satan to consider the life of Job, he said of his faithful servant, "Still he holds fast to his integrity, although you incited Me against him, to destroy him without cause" (Job 2:3). But this time, Satan said that if Job's body was afflicted, he would surely curse God (Job 2:5).

And the LORD said to Satan, "Behold, he is in your hand, but spare his life." So Satan went out from the presence of the LORD, and struck Job with painful boils from the sole of his foot to the crown of his head. (Job 2:6-7)

From Job 2:8–37:24, the Bible gives the account of a season of time during which Job experienced the divine discipline of *divine darkness*. The story of Job had a happy ending, but before the last chapter was written, Job had come to the end of himself. He never cursed God, but he cursed the day of his birth. Job got so low in his life that he exclaimed, "Why did I not die at birth?" (Job 3:11).

THE DIVINE DISCIPLINE OF DARKNESS

Job has been used as an example to introduce the divine discipline of darkness. Job used the word *darkness* to describe the "adversity" (Job 2:10) God had sent upon him:

He has fenced up my way, so that I cannot pass; and He has set darkness in my paths. (Job 19:8)

Because I was not cut off from the presence of darkness, and He did not hide deep darkness from my face. (Job 23:17)

But when I looked for good, evil came to me; and when I waited for light, then came darkness. (Job 30:26)

Several words from the Hebrew and Greek are translated into English as "darkness." The meaning can either be literal or figurative. Context determines whether its usage is for physical darkness or spiritual darkness. Two different Hebrew words are used in Job for darkness. Both of these words appear in Job 23:17. The first use in the verse is the word *chosek*. Literally, it means a state that is the opposite of light. Figuratively, it means distress, blindness, or judgment. The second word translated "darkness" is *ophel*. Literally, it refers to a deep darkness which is so dark, that you cannot see anything. Figuratively, it means spiritual darkness as a result of a calamity. The figurative meaning applies for both words in Job 23:17, but the literal sense of the words helps to bring out the spiritual picture Job was trying to make. Job has implied in this verse that he was not spared from adversity coming upon him and that God did not protect him from the calamities which resulted in his state of spiritual darkness.

OTHER BIBLICAL EXAMPLES OF DIVINE DARKNESS

Although Job will be the main example of divine darkness, other biblical examples give an insight into the divine discipline of darkness. Jeremiah, the "weeping prophet," was one whom God used to speak an unpopular message of judgment and doom. Jeremiah experienced divine darkness in his life. He said about God, "He has led me and made me walk in darkness and not in light" (Lam. 3:2). This was the one to whom God had said, "For you shall go to all to whom I send you, and whatever I command you, you shall speak. Do not be afraid of their faces, for I am with you to deliver you" (Jer. 1:7-8).

Isaiah made a reference that is applicable to the divine discipline of divine darkness: "Who among you fears the LORD? Who obeys the voice of His Servant? Who walks in darkness and has no light? Let him trust in the name of the LORD and rely upon his God" (Isa. 50:10).

In 2 Samuel 22:29-32, David proclaimed, "For You are my lamp, O LORD; the LORD shall enlighten my darkness. For by You I can run against a troop; by my God I can leap over a wall. As for God, His way is perfect; the word of the LORD is proven; He is a shield to all who trust in Him." This scripture passage contains the words of a song that David wrote after "the Lord delivered him from the hand of all his enemies, and from the hand of Saul" (2 Sam. 22:1). David was the one described by God as "a man after my own heart, who will do all my will" (Acts 13:22; also 1 Sam. 13:14). Now he was not without faults and failures in his life, even being guilty of adultery and part of a murder plot, but the divine darkness that David experienced was not punishment for sin, it was divine discipline to mold David into a man after God's own heart who would do all his will.

The prophet Micah knew about divine darkness when he wrote, "Do not rejoice over me, my enemy; when I fall, I will arise; When I sit in darkness, the Lord will be a light to me" (Micah 7:8).

DIVINE DARKNESS TRAINS US TO HEAR GOD

God may put you in a state of spiritual darkness. When God has placed divine darkness upon you, you know it. You know God is there, and you can even be calling upon God daily, spending a great amount of time doing so, but you just cannot seem to find his will or direction concerning various matters of your life. God has his purposes for sending divine darkness, but it is a tough discipline to endure. It takes a mature Christian to be exercised by it because a weaker Christian might become so discouraged in it that he may waver in his faith or be tossed to and fro so that he would miss the reason for the divine darkness.

Among the reasons why God sends divine darkness is that he uses it to *train us to hear Him*. We live in a day when we are bombarded from all sides by well-intentioned individuals with sincere advice as to how we should respond to decisions facing us. But the voice we must hear above all others regarding the issues of life is the voice of God. We are often put into the "shadow of God's hand," as Oswald Chambers described it, until we learn to hear him above all else and all others.

> *So often, God's direction for a particular matter will lead us to do what is contrary to our human logic.*

When we have decisions to make, whether they are major ones or minor ones, God wants to lead us to make the right choice. Human nature leads us to make the common sense decision. That is where most of our advice from others will lead us. But so often, God's direction for a particular matter will lead us to do what is contrary to our human logic. It is often the opposite of what would seem the normal thing to do. The Bible says, "Trust in the LORD with all your heart, And lean not on your own understanding" (Prov. 3:5). God wants us to lean on his understanding. That is why we are to know his voice. It is so that we will follow him (John 10:4), and that we will not be directed incorrectly by the voice of a stranger (John 10:5). To follow the wrong advice is to follow the voice of a stranger.

From the life of Job, we learn three results God desires in our lives as he uses divine darkness to train us to hear him. We are to (1) seek God's voice above all others; (2) stay upon God until you hear his voice; and (3) speak God's message in the light.

SEEK GOD'S VOICE ABOVE ALL OTHERS

If divine darkness comes upon you, *seek God's voice above all others.* Divine darkness is the time to listen to God's voice alone. One reason why God may put you in the dark is because too many voices have been influencing you, and you are having a hard time distinguishing the voice of God from others. As a result, you may be about to make a wrong move, or you may have already gotten started in the wrong direction. So God places you in divine darkness so that you will seek his voice above all others.

When you find yourself in the spiritual dark, you need to *be still.* It is a time to think back to where you believe God put you into darkness. Review the decisions you were facing at the time. If you are not definitely sure that you acted according to the will of God, then halt as much as possible in the situation and circumstances you are in right now. When all the adversity came upon Job, he halted everything. He sat for seven days and seven nights, not saying a word to anybody, and no one spoke a word to him (Job 2:13). It was a great time of grief for Job, but surely, as he sat still and silent, he reviewed every decision of his life that he could remember.

As you review decisions and realize that you made some poor decisions, then reverse those decisions as God permits, as it is appropriate, and in an ethical manner. Several years ago, a pastor left a strong, solid church he had pastored for several years to accept the pastorate of what was then a larger, more well-known church in another state. After a few weeks on the new church field, he felt that he had missed the will of God in moving to that church. He was completely honest about it with the members of the church, and in a spirit of understanding they accepted his resignation. His former church asked him if he would come back as their pastor. He did, and the church flourished, grew, and received notoriety for its ministries.

Sometimes, though, decisions cannot be reversed immediately. For instance, a student may enter a college and later realize he needs to be at another school that would better fit him for continuing his education. But he would be better off finishing a semester of school, without loss of course credits and tuition, before transferring to the college where he really needs to be.

Then there are decisions that are irreversible once they have been made. For example, you should not reverse a decision if you have to

28

violate a scriptural truth or principle. *God will never call us to disobey his Word to obey his will.* In such a case, when a decision cannot be changed, ask God to help you live so that you can serve him, even though you missed his will regarding that decision. Make a fresh commitment to live within his will from that point on in your life.

When you are in divine darkness, you not only need to be still in seeking God's voice above all others, but you need to *be silent* as much as possible about your situation. If you talk very much in the dark, especially about why you may be in it, you normally will talk in the wrong mood, in a spirit of anger, bitterness, confusion, fear, frustration, or worry. For seven days and seven nights, Job was silent (Job 2:13), when divine darkness came sweeping over his life. The Bible says that in all the adversity which came upon Job, he did not sin with his lips (Job 2:10). His silence, early in his state of divine darkness, was a factor to his not sinning with his lips. Now the Lord did acknowledge that Job spoke some things that revealed a lack of knowledge and understanding (Job 38:1-3), but Job never denied his faith in God.

> *God will never call us to disobey his Word to obey his will.*

In the spiritual dark, be cautious whom you seek out to talk to about your situation or whom you accept counsel from. God does use people to speak his will for us, but in divine darkness, it is extremely important to be cautious. You need someone who will not simply tell you what you want to hear because they don't want to hurt your feelings. It needs to be someone who, in speaking what they believe to be the will of God, will be honest and pointed with you, even though it may be hard for you to hear and heed. And in some cases, you may just need to wait and be silent and pray the Lord sends someone to give you his counsel. Oswald Chambers observed,

> *We are put into the shadow of God's hand until we learn to hear Him. . . . Watch where God puts you into darkness, and when you are there keep your mouth shut. Are you in the dark just now in your circumstances, or in your life with God? Then remain quiet. If you open your mouth in the dark, you will talk in the wrong mood: darkness is the time to listen. Don't talk to other people about it;*

don't read books to find out the reason of the darkness, but listen and heed. If you talk to other people, you cannot hear what God is saying. When you are in the dark, listen, and God will give you a very precious message for someone else when you get into the light.[2]

Also consider that *God can say as much in his silence as he says when he speaks.* Silence can speak louder than words. When you clear out the noise and clutter of other voices, your spiritual ears can clearly hear the voice of God. And if God continues to remain silent, your spiritual mental perception will be sharper when you get away from the clutter of other voices. God will not necessarily need to speak to you because you will be able to perceive where you got off course of his will. Seek God's voice and his vision for your life above all else.

In Job's period of divine darkness, he had some well-intentioned friends who came to be with him during his suffering. They all offered their opinion as to why God had put divine darkness upon Job. But none of those four men said what God wanted Job to hear. The four men were sincere in their efforts to help their friend, Job, but they were sincerely wrong. They all had some wise things to say, especially Elihu, the last one to speak. But none completely represented God in what he wanted to say to Job (Job 42:7). *Sincerity can be sincerely wrong.*

> *God can say as much in his silence as he says when he speaks.*

When you are in divine darkness, seek God's voice above all others. In going back to where God put you into divine darkness, if you find that you made a wrong move, then correct your situation as much as you are able by God's direction. If you believe that you have made decisions within the will of God, then be silent, remain quiet, and listen for the voice of God.

Job got to the point where he desperately wanted to hear the voice of God:

Oh, that I knew where I might find Him, That I might come to His seat! I would present my case before Him, And fill my mouth with

---

2.   Ibid., 32.

arguments. I would know the words which He would answer me,
And understand what He would say to me. (Job 23:3-5)

Job did come to an understanding of what God had to say to him, but he heard it when he listened for and to the voice of God alone.

STAY UPON GOD UNTIL YOU HEAR HIS VOICE

In spiritual darkness, not only should you seek God's voice above all others by being silent and still, but you also need to *stay upon God until you hear his voice.* The prophet Isaiah said,

> *Who is among you that feareth the LORD, that obeyeth the voice of his servant, that walketh in darkness, and hath no light? let him trust in the name of the LORD, and stay upon his God. (Isa. 50:10 KJV)*

The Hebrew word translated "stay" in the King James Version of the Bible of Isaiah 50:10 literally means "lean" or "support oneself" on something. This same word is translated "lean" in Proverbs 3:5, which says, "Trust in the LORD with all your heart, and lean not on your own understanding." In Proverbs 3:5, the application of this verse is that you lean to God's understanding by placing absolute trust and confidence in him so that no matter how difficult a situation you may be experiencing, you will not take matters into your own hands, but you will wait on God to see you through. In divine darkness, you are not to take matters into your own hands, and you are not to trust man's understanding with your life's plan. How can you do that? You are to stay upon God by *leaning on his Word.* In the midst of divine darkness, Job said, "I have not departed from the commandment of His lips; I have treasured the words of His mouth more than my necessary food" (Job 23:12). The means by which you lean upon the Word of God today is through the Bible. It is the only book that you really need to read when you are in divine darkness.

As you stay upon God by leaning upon his Word, *look for your word from God in the Word,* when you are experiencing divine discipline. As you look, listen at the same time. God has a message for you that you can only find and confirm in the Bible. Now there are other ways other than the Bible by which God speaks to us and directs us, but none of those ways will ever be in contradiction or disagreement with the scriptures. If they are, you can be assured that you are not hearing the voice of God.

In divine darkness, you are to stay true to those divinely inspired autographs, written by God through about forty individuals over a period of fifteen hundred years, which became the Bible as we know it. You will find and hear your word from God through a verse or passage that will stir your heart and soul regarding your particular situation. Job stayed upon God by leaning upon God's Word alone. Chapters 38–41 record God's Word for Job.

The only possibility of fully understanding the ways and works of the Lord is by the Word of God within you (John 16:13). The Bible has many words to us, but in divine darkness, look and listen for a word from the Word. There are times when a specific verse or passage of the scriptures will stir you. Those words become the word from the Word for you in the particular condition you are in. That is the way God speaks to us today.

The prophet Isaiah said of God, "Your counsels of old are faithfulness and truth (Isa. 25:1). Those "counsels of old" are just as faithful and true for today as they ever have been. Isaiah also said of God, "You will keep him in perfect peace, whose mind is stayed on You" (Isa. 26:3). You can be at peace in the spiritual dark as you stay upon God by leaning on and looking to his Word until you hear his voice. God will speak to you by the simple way of words, as spoken through the Holy scriptures, and as stirred by the "still, small voice" of the Holy Spirit.

Speak God's Message In the Light

When God speaks to you in the spiritual dark, it is not something you are to keep only within yourself and for yourself. God's message to you is also a message for others that they need to hear. When you get back into the spiritual light, you must *speak God's message in the light*. Jesus said, "Whatever I tell you in the dark, speak in the light" (Matt. 10:27). There are two benefits that God's message to you in the dark will have for others: enlightenment and encouragement. The Bible says in Psalm 18:28, "For you will light my lamp; The Lord my God will enlighten my darkness." God's message to you in divine darkness is for your *enlightenment* and the enlightenment of others. Job had a greater message to share after his period of divine darkness. It was an enlightenment not only to himself, but also to others, especially Eliphaz, Bildad, and Zophar (see Job 42:7-9). The enlightenment received from divine darkness is beneficial in two ways: unto salvation and unto sanctification.

When Paul was converted on the road to Damascus, the commission of the Lord Jesus to Paul was for him to take the gospel to all the world "to open their eyes, in order to turn them from darkness to light, and from the power of Satan to God, that they may receive forgiveness of sins and an inheritance among those who are sanctified by faith in Me" (Acts 26:18). Divine darkness gets you completely set apart to God, to the point that you realize nothing in life matters more than your personal salvation from sin through Christ. Everything you have—property, possessions, prosperity, your family—can be taken from you, but your eternal salvation cannot be taken (Rom. 6:23; Eph. 2:8-9).

> *Divine darkness reduces you to nothing so much so that you are so hungry to hear God that everything else fades out of view.*

I mentioned in the first chapter that sometimes God may have to reduce you to nothing so that he becomes your everything in order that he can do anything he wants to do through you. Divine darkness reduces you to nothing so much so that you are so hungry to hear God that everything else fades out of view. The enlightenment received is then for your benefit. It is then that the Lord can light your lamp and enlighten your darkness. It is then that you can most effectively become the light of the world in the spiritual darkness around you. Your light begins to shine before men so that they may see your good works and many will be led to glorify your Father in heaven (Matt. 5:16). As a result, your divine darkness has enlightened others unto the salvation of their souls.

You and I are chosen to "proclaim the praises of Him who called us out of darkness into His marvelous light" (1 Pet. 2:9). As nothing matters more than your own salvation from sin, you have a desire to lead others to Christ. You become a "vessel of honor, sanctified and useful for the Master" (2 Tim. 2:21) as you desire to live a life of obedience and commitment to the Lord because you want to live before those to whom you witness a living example of what it is to be a Christian. Your enlightenment is then for the benefit of others in that they too may be saved from the darkness of sin and sanctified also to shine as lights in the moral and spiritual darkness around us. As you are already saved, divine darkness leads you to become more holy so that others may be saved and set apart as witnesses for the Lord.

When you are in divine darkness, God's message to you is also *for the encouragement of others*. The Bible says that we are mutually encouraged by each other's faith (Rom. 1:12). As other Christians, particularly weaker Christians, see you remain committed to the Lord and to your faith while you are in divine darkness, it is an encouragement to them. It prepares them to receive divine discipline from the Lord for its intended purpose, not as punishment, but as a means of taking them from a weak faith to a strong, mature faith. The message you have received, and your remaining faithful while waiting to receive it, help to strengthen weaker Christians.

The message God gives you in the spiritual dark may also be for the purpose of encouragement in edifying, reconfirming, and directing believers to greater maturity. Your message from God is also meant to stir willing Christians who will receive it and respond to it. God has his special spokesmen in every generation who can so open the scriptures to us that our hearts burn within us (Luke 24:32). These spokesmen make God's wonderful counsels of old (Isa. 25:1) wonderful counsels for today. They bring fresh insights and deeper understanding into verses and passages we have heard preached upon many times before. Divine darkness is one way God gives such powerful messages to these proclaimers of the Word who stir our hearts and lives to change and who move us to higher levels of faith. Such sermons are born in the dark, still night of the soul, when all you can focus your sight on is God, and the only sounds you hear are from God. If it were not for the night, we would never know the sparkling brightness, brilliance, and beauty the light of the stars produces. It is a unique kind of light from that which we see in the daytime. It is never too bright for the eyes to gaze upon, but peaceful and pleasant to behold. There are truths, lessons, experiences, and wonders of the Christian life that would never be seen, heard, or learned if we were always in the light concerning all spiritual matters. Be thankful for those who have shared the message they have learned and heard in the spiritual dark; otherwise, you may never have known it.

CONCLUSION

Divine darkness trains us to hear God. This comes through seeking God's voice above all others, staying upon God until you hear his voice, and then speaking the message God has given you to others who need to hear it in the light. Job did in divine darkness what he needed to do, and he came out of it a better and greater man. He sought God's voice above all others. He did not heed the voice of strangers (John 10:5)—in his case, some well-intentioned friends who offered plenty of advice. Job stayed upon God until he heard God's voice. He got to the point that he desperately wanted to hear from God, so much that he hungered for the Word of God more than food. He treasured God's words as the most valuable thing he could receive (Job 23:12). He heard from God, and he knew it when God spoke to him.

The book of Job begins by revealing what a great man of God Job was. The book of Job ends with Job an even greater man of God. But he had to go through an extremely dark period to be that greater man for God. Job already knew much about God before his season of divine darkness. He knew enough about God that he had a healthy fear, reverence, and awe of the Lord. But through the divine darkness he experienced, Job really got to know God intimately:

> *I know that You can do everything, And that no purpose of Yours can be withheld from You. You asked, "Who is this who hides counsel without knowledge?" Therefore I have uttered what I did not understand, Things too wonderful for me, which I did not know. Listen, please, and let me speak; You said, "I will question you, and you shall answer Me." I have heard of You by the hearing of the ear, But now my eye sees You. Therefore I abhor myself, And repent in dust and ashes. (Job 42:2-6)*

Those are the words of a man who not only knew of God, about God, and who believed in God; those are the words of a man who personally and intimately knew God, heart to heart. The divine darkness Isaiah and Jeremiah experienced factored into the powerful prophecies they proclaimed under the inspiration of God. They were men who knew God personally and intimately. Certainly the divine darkness David experienced helped influence the book of Psalms and so many verses and passages that minister to us concerning the issues of life, because every emotion we feel is in those psalms. David was a man who knew God personally and intimately, and God himself said about David that he was a man after God's own heart. Like Job, divine darkness was the discipline by which Isaiah, Jeremiah, David, Micah, and others heard clearly the only voice that mattered, the voice of God, which they boldly proclaimed to those who needed to hear God's message. Through it all, God gave a message to Job that benefitted Job personally, that was the salvation of Job's friends (Job 42:7-9), and that is an encouraging and inspirational message for us today. It is a message which we can look to as we strive to endure dark and difficult times. If God should bring divine darkness upon us, may it be as spiritually profitable to us as was the divine darkness of Job.

3: DIVINE DARKNESS

"TEACHING US TO HEED GOD"

Divine Darkness: A state in which God places one in a period of extended, mostly private meditation for the purpose of producing deeper fellowship with God in order to reveal the powerful spiritual insights gleaned during this time.

After these things the word of the LORD came to Abram in a vision, saying, "Do not be afraid, Abram. I am your shield, your exceedingly great reward." But Abram said, "Lord GOD, what will You give me, seeing I go childless, and the heir of my house is Eliezer of Damascus?" Then Abram said, "Look, You have given me no offspring; indeed one born in my house is my heir!" And behold, the word of the LORD came to him, saying, "This one shall not be your heir, but one who will come from your own body shall be your heir." (Gen. 15:1-4)

God was very clear in what he told Abraham: "From your own body shall be your heir" (Gen. 15:4). Abraham would have his own son to be the heir of all that God had given him and promised to give him. The Lord further stated that Abraham's descendants would be as numerous as the stars above (Gen. 15:5). And the Bible records that Abraham "believed in the Lord, and He accounted it to him for righteousness" (Gen. 15:6). Abraham knew what God had said to him. God had given him a message, but then, Abraham was put into the "shadow of God's hand."

DIVINE DARKNESS TEACHES US TO HEED GOD

A purpose of divine darkness is to train us to hear God. But there is a step that must follow hearing God. We must respond in obedience to what God has spoken to us. *Divine darkness also teaches us to heed God.* Obedience to God is doing exactly what God says to do, when he says to do it, with the proper attitude. We normally do not develop such character in our lives until we have come completely to the end of ourselves so that we trust God completely, knowing that he is faithful to do what he will do. We will hear and heed God when we have an unswaying, confident hope in his Word and in his will for our lives.

> *We normally do not develop such character in our lives until we have come completely to the end of ourselves so that we trust God completely, knowing that he is faithful to do what he says he will do.*

Sometimes, when God speaks to you, whether his message is mostly for your benefit or for the benefit of others, it may not be God's will for you to make the message known immediately. Or he may have you to make the message known, yet the fulfillment of it may not happen for a long time. The fulfillment of the message may be preceded by a season of darkness. In both cases, God has his reasons for it. One of the reasons may be that you are not ready. Another reason may be that others who are going to hear the message are not ready. But in his time, God will bring it about. You can be sure that God knows what is going on and that he is getting everything in proper order. For the process of divine darkness to teach you to heed God, you must wait for the Father and work without faltering; but, in the process, you will learn to walk by faith.

WAIT FOR THE FATHER

When God has spoken to you and given you a vision of something he wants to do for you or through you, but darkness follows, *wait for your heavenly Father* before you proceed forward with the revelation. It could be that God needs to get you fit by making you in accordance with the Word he has given you, which he will fulfill, if you wait on his timing.

The period of time that you wait for the Father could be for years, for just a few months, or for a shorter period of time. There is a process by which God has to get you ready, and he has to get others ready who are going to hear his message through you. Then, when things are just right, God puts everything into proper order.

I sensed the call of God for me to preach, and to be a pastor of a church, four years before it actually became reality. At the time of my call, I had been serving churches full time as a minister of youth for several years and taking seminary courses on the side. But when the call came, I felt that there was still some getting fit on my part that the Lord desired. So, as a thirty-six-year-old married man with two children, I resigned my church staff position and entered seminary full time. Three years later, I graduated with a master of divinity degree.

It took another ten months after graduating from seminary before I began my first pastorate. Those ten months seemed as long as the three years it took to complete my seminary degree. I was ready to pastor, but God had to get me right for the church field he had for me. And he had to get the church right for calling me to be their pastor. While getting my seminary degree I began working part time as singles director at my home church, and I was put on as the full-time minister of singles a few months later. My home church was in a growth boom when I became part of the ministerial staff. One year we reached a level that only forty-one other churches in the Southern Baptist Convention attained of baptizing over a hundred with at least a 10 percent numerical increase in average Sunday school attendance.

I liked a big church. I felt comfortable and at home being a member and staff member of a big church. But God had different plans for my future. He had to get me right for leaving a church with over three thousand members for one with just over four hundred members. He had to get me right for going from a church with eight full-time ministerial staff members to a church where I was the only full-time staff member. Are you getting the picture? It took several months, but God, in his usual and unusual ways, had the situation so right for me to be called as pastor of Dixie Lee Baptist Church that I considered it the greatest honor of my life when this church extended the call to me. And it was a wonderful relationship between this pastor and that church during the three years I served there. But it took time to get us ready and right for one another.

GETTING FIT TO FULFILL GOD'S WILL TAKES TIME

When God's will is fulfilled in your life, it will *testify to the truth* of the message he gave you earlier. But it requires your waiting for the Father to bring about what he has spoken to you. The life of Jeremiah shows a positive example of one who waited for the Father. He knew from firsthand experience that God's Word was not always fulfilled immediately. But he learned from experience that God would always come through. He was able to testify, "The LORD has done what He purposed; He has fulfilled His word Which He commanded in days of old" (Lam. 2:17).

A Positive Example: Jeremiah

The "weeping prophet" was one whom God used to speak an unpopular message of judgment and doom. Jeremiah experienced divine darkness in his life. He said about God, "He has led me and made me walk in darkness and not in light" (Lam. 3:2). This was the one to whom God had said, "For you shall go to all to whom I send you, and whatever I command you, you shall speak. Do not be afraid of their faces, For I am with you to deliver you" (Jer. 1:7-8).

Jeremiah expected deliverance, but he often encountered delay. This led to difficult times for him. His prophecies and messages to a people who were disobedient to God led to his suffering persecution. God had promised to take care of Jeremiah and to deliver him from those who were the recipients of the prophet's unpopular messages and ministry. There were times, though, when he waited long periods of time for deliverance. During such times, Jeremiah felt like he was a laughingstock of the people as they mocked him. He said, "I am in derision daily; everyone mocks me" (Jer. 20:7). They did so because he would sometimes give a message of judgment and doom, which did not come true immediately. So they made fun of the "foolish" prophet's "crazy" predictions. It got so bad that Jeremiah wanted to quit. He expressed depression, as recorded in Jeremiah 20:8-9, when he said, "The word of the LORD was made to me a reproach and a derision daily. Then I said, 'I will not make mention of Him, nor speak anymore in His name.' But His word was in my heart like a burning fire shut up in my bones; I was weary of holding it back, And I could not."

Preaching the message of God was a difficult task for Jeremiah, but he endured the difficulty. He would have preferred for the people to have been faithful and obedient to God than his having to preach messages of judgment and doom. He did not want his country to be invaded by foreigners, with his people being captured and exiled from their land. Yet Jeremiah had been called by God to speak for God to the people for their good, but they either resented him or they did not believe him. Still, through it all, Jeremiah exhibited dedication in speaking for God.

In the same lament in which Jeremiah referred to the darkness into which God had led him, he also acknowledged that God leads in the darkness. No matter what, Jeremiah expressed that he would wait for his Father to deliver him: "The LORD is good to those who wait for Him, to the soul who seeks Him. It is good that one should hope and wait quietly For the salvation of the LORD" (Lam. 3:25-26). Jeremiah had been taught by God to heed God, regardless of what happened. That process often required waiting for the heavenly Father to do what he said he would do.

A Poor Example: Abraham

In Abraham's situation, he heard God, but he did not heed God by waiting for his heavenly Father to bring about what God had spoken to him. There was a period of time in his life when Abraham was a poor example of waiting for the Father. In Genesis 15:4, God told Abraham that he would have a son. The sixteenth chapter of Genesis illustrates what happens when you do not wait for God and his means of provision.

After God had initially spoken to Abraham concerning his heir-to-be, Abraham later listened to what he thought was sound advice, but it was actually bad advice. It came from his wife, regarding her idea of how to become parents. Sarah suggested that she give her Egyptian maid, Hagar, to Abraham to bear a child on Sarah's behalf, for their culture allowed a barren woman to do that. The Bible says, "And Abram heeded the voice of Sarai" (Gen. 16:2). Abraham did not wait for God, and he listened to the wrong advice.

When Abraham was eighty-six years old, Hagar bore a son for Abraham and Sarah, whom they named Ishmael. But it was not done God's way. The result led to wrathful actions. There was a brief period of contention between Abraham and Sarah (Gen. 16:5), but it caused a permanent conflict between Sarah and Hagar (Gen. 16:6; 21:9-10, 14). As God had promised a son to Abraham and Sarah, their own son, Isaac, was born to Sarah, although it was not until thirteen years after the birth of Ishmael. Sarah, then, did not want Ishmael around Isaac, so she eventually had Hagar and Ishmael thrown out of their family compound. What a mess it caused for Abraham and his family because he did not wait for God to fulfill what he had promised to do, in his time and in his way.

> *Never try to help God fulfill his Word in the logic of the flesh.*

When God speaks a message to you, and darkness follows, wait for the Father before you act in response to the message. Never try to help God fulfill his Word in the logic of the flesh. Abraham looked to weak answers to fulfill the desire that he and Sarah had—to have their own child—because they looked to the logic of the flesh more than they trusted the absolute dependability of the Word of God. Sarah thought that at seventy-five years of age, she was too old to bear a child. Since their custom allowed her maid to bear a child by Abraham that would legally be Sarah's baby, they chose that weak answer as the means by which to have a child. The result of Abraham's listening to the wrong advice and looking to weak answers, while he was in divine darkness, resulted in bitterness, jealousy, chaos, confusion, and hurt. Such wrathful actions are never the will of God.

We must always let God bring about his Word in his way and in his time. If we will wait for the Father to bring about what he has spoken to us, the fulfillment of it gives testimony that his Word is truth. And you can be sure that his Word will be executed and completed when everything is in proper order.

WORK WITHOUT FALTERING

As you wait for the Father to bring about the message he has spoken to you, it does not mean that you are to become, as an old saying goes, "so heavenly minded, you're no earthly good." While waiting for the next step of action within the will of God concerning his Word to you, there is enough to do in the general will of God to keep you busy until then. You are not to drop everything so that you become spiritually stagnant until you receive your next move from God. The key is to *work without faltering*. To falter means to lose courage, to hesitate, to retreat, to waver, to stumble, or to move unsteadily. God has his reasons for keeping you in spiritual darkness after you have heard his voice regarding a particular matter. You just need to continue to do his work, without faltering. You will still be able to effectively serve him in the darkness, as well as shine for him in the darkness.

In the spiritual dark, you are to continue the normal work for the Lord that every Christian ought to be doing faithfully, regardless of circumstances. You can usefully *serve Him in the darkness*. Your main responsibility, as you serve the Lord in divine darkness, is to keep from losing heart, from losing courage, and from wavering spiritually in the process.

As you wait upon further directions from God, as was mentioned in the previous chapter, stay upon God's Word. It is a time to continue being a "doer of the word" (James 1:22) and a "doer of the work" (James 1:25) of the Lord. It will keep you from faltering, and it will be a source of encouragement for you. The Bible says in James 1:25, "But he who looks into the perfect law of liberty and continues in it, and is not a forgetful hearer but a doer of the work, this one will be blessed in what he does." As you continue to serve him in the darkness by leaning upon the Word and by doing his work, you will be personally blessed through the joy, peace, and satisfaction that comes in doing the will of God, no matter what you are facing.

In the first chapter of James, the Bible also says that you ought to "count it all joy when you fall into various trials, knowing that the testing of your faith produces patience" (James 1:2-3). The Bible is full of examples of those who learned patience and exhibited patience through trials and testings—Abraham, Moses, David, Elijah, Jeremiah, Jesus, and Paul, just to name a few. During divine darkness, to keep from faltering and to patiently wait for the Father, you must be a doer of his Word. You learn to do his Word by delighting in his Word. Even in divine darkness, the Bible will continue to be a lamp unto your feet and a light unto your path (Ps. 119:105). As you delight in God's Word, it will lead you to do his Word, and as you do his Word, you do the work that God has willed for you.

Where God may put you into spiritual darkness concerning one area of your life, or regarding a particular issue of life, does not necessarily put you into darkness in all areas of your life. For example, a minister may sense that God is about to move him to another church or to another area of ministry. That does not mean that the minister should back off or neglect his present place of ministry and do any less than his best for the Lord where he is presently serving. I heard a statement several years ago that is so applicable to such situations: "I would rather be doing the right *what* of the will of God in the wrong *where,* than to be doing the wrong *what* in the right *where* of the will of God." You do his work by doing his Word. As you delight in his Word, you will delight in his work and patiently endure the dark, unknown areas of your life until God brings light into those areas.

It is even possible for you to *shine in the darkness.* The psalmist said, "If I say, 'Surely the darkness shall fall on me,' even the night shall be light about me; indeed, the darkness shall not hide from You, but the night shines as the day; the darkness and the light are both alike to You" (Ps. 139:11-12). God sees you in the dark and he recognizes you. He can shine through you and around you in the spiritual darkness, but only if you continue in his work without faltering.

It will be difficult much of the time that you are in divine darkness to continue to do his work without faltering. You may even feel, at times, that your "way is hidden from the Lord" (Isa. 40:28). But "the everlasting God, the Lord, the Creator of the ends of the earth" (Isa. 40:28), the all-seeing, all-knowing heavenly Father will give wisdom, understanding, power, and strength, in his time, to those who wait for him. Divine darkness is a time that God uses as a means to bring spiritual renewal and revival into your life. The Bible says, "But those who wait on the LORD shall renew their strength; they shall mount up with wings like eagles, they shall run and not be weary, they shall walk and not faint" (Isa. 40:31). One songwriter has described the importance of waiting on the Lord this way:

> *But good things come to them that wait, not to those who hesitate,*
> *So hurry up and wait upon the Lord.*
> *More power to ya, when you're standing on His Word;*
> *When you're trusting with your whole heart in the message you have heard.*
> *More power to ya, when we're all in one accord;*
> *They that wait upon the Lord, they shall renew, they shall renew their*
> *strength.*[3]

You can shine divine darkness for the Lord because he recognizes you and also because he uses divine darkness as a time to spiritually renew and ripen (mature) you. It is a time to wait for the Father, but also, to continue working for him while you wait for his will to be fulfilled. You can patiently endure it by showing complete trust in the Lord, staying true to his Word, and steadily serving him where you are. *The God who disciplines you will also deliver you, in his time.* God removes you from the spiritual dark when he knows the time is right for you and for others who will benefit from the purpose of your divine darkness.

If the spiritual situation which has been described thus far in this chapter applies to you, let this biblical exhortation, encouragement, and challenge guide you:

> *Roll your works onto the Lord, trust in Him, rest in the Lord, and wait patiently for Him by delighting in His Word. Continue working for Him, without faltering, and He shall bring to pass the message He has spoken to you. Your thoughts will be established His way, the Lord will direct your steps, and He will bring you forth from out of the darkness into the light. (Paraphrased from Ps. 37:5-7; Prov. 16:3, 9)*

Walk By Faith

As you have waited for the Father and continued to work without faltering, when God brings you out of the spiritual dark, the result is that you will have matured in learning to *walk by faith.* James exhorted us

---

3. Bob Hartman, *More Power To Ya*, Dawn Treader Music, 1982.

to count it a joy when experiencing trials, testing, and tribulation, for as you learn to trust God to see you through, you will become mature and complete in your faith (James 1:2-4).

As you learn to walk by faith, *it matures your personal testimony for Christ.* You develop patience and perseverance through waiting on God to bring you out of divine darkness, in his way and in his time. To endure patiently and faithfully through adverse times is a powerful witness, when compared to the normal emotions of fear, frustration, a sense of failure, or falling apart emotionally. Endurance is a sign of mature faith.

Peter exhorted us in his second epistle to give all diligence to "add to your faith virtue, to virtue knowledge, to knowledge self-control, to self-control perseverance, to perseverance godliness, to godliness brotherly kindness, and to brotherly kindness love. For if these things are yours and abound, you will be neither barren nor unfruitful in the knowledge of our Lord Jesus Christ" (2 Pet. 1:5-8). We are to live by faith, not by sight, and there are characteristics that should be in our lives to give evidence of our faith. James and Peter have given us some of those evident characteristics of a mature faith. In the Bible, clouds are connected with God. To the Israelites on the exodus from Egypt, a cloud represented the presence, direction, and protection of God (Ex. 13:21; 14:19-20). To the praying Elijah, on top of Mount Carmel, the clouds, along with the wind and heavy rain, were evidence of the presence and provision of God (1 Kings 18:44-45). The "clouds of life" do not normally have the awesome "power of God effect" on our lives as those literal examples from the time of Moses and Elijah, but they are a sign from the Lord that he is there. Oswald Chambers said,

> *Clouds are those sorrows or sufferings or providences, within or without our personal lives, which seem to dispute the rule of God. It is by those very clouds that the Spirit of God is teaching us how to walk by faith. If there were no clouds, we should have no faith. "The clouds are but the dust of our Father's feet." The clouds are a sign that He is there. What a revelation it is to know that sorrow and bereavement and suffering are the clouds that come along with God! God cannot come near without the clouds.*[4]

---

4. Chambers, *My Utmost for His Highest*, 153.

Divine darkness is a dark time! It seems like a dark cloud is hanging over you. But those clouds let you know that God is there. In divine darkness, you see *the presence of God manifested upon your life* as you learn to walk by faith, trusting him for direction, protection, and provision. Divine darkness is not an easy discipline of the Lord to endure. Clouds are a good picture of what it is like in the midst of divine darkness. You cannot see very clearly, you must move very cautiously, and you long to hear from God. But this is where *the power of God is magnified in your life.*

God gave a promise to Abraham: "You're going to have a child from your own body." But it was not initially done God's way. It was thirteen years before God revealed to Abraham that his heir would come according to God's design for child-bearing, through Sarah, Abraham's wife. The promise of God was fulfilled in Sarah's bearing a son, but they faltered earlier in the process and turned to common sense logic. They did not patiently wait for God. They did it their way. It caused a mess! But God said that he was going to do something, and when we blow it, God will straighten things out as we get back into his will for our lives. And that is when we can see the power of God magnified in our lives. He will still accomplish what he has said he will do, in spite of the complications we have caused. God is bigger than any problem we have. But we must trust his way and his timing in the fulfillment of his will.

A famous line from the movie *Miracle On 34th Street* is the statement, "Faith is believing in something when common sense tells you not to." Common sense logic told Abraham and Sarah that she was too old to bear a child. Faith called on them to trust and believe in God, in spite of all the circumstances. That is when his power is magnified in your life (2 Cor. 12:9).

> *God is bigger than any problem we have. But we must trust his way and his timing in the fulfillment of his will.*

Another positive result of divine darkness is that *it mobilizes the purpose of God for your life.* When it exercises you according to the line of quality that God wants in your life, you are ready and willing to do his will. Abraham learned his lesson from divine darkness. During the thirteen years of darkness, and the mess that came about because he yielded to common sense, Abraham learned to completely heed God. When a son came God's way, the future possibility of relying on common sense logic over faith was no longer an option. Abraham learned to lean completely on God.

Years later, a great test came upon the now mature and complete faith of Abraham. The Hall of Faith chapter in Hebrews confirms that Abraham had learned to heed God's voice: "By faith Abraham, when he was tested, offered up Isaac, and he who had received the promises offered up his only begotten son" (Heb. 11:17). But the Lord provided deliverance for Abraham (Gen. 22:14). He had learned to look to God for the answers (Gen. 22:12-13). In the process, Abraham learned liberation in his soul over the weakness of the flesh, as he developed a faith to completely trust God for all the needs and concerns of life. He reached a level of faith that did not question the will of God and that would wait for God to work, in his time and in his way.

CONCLUSION

Divine darkness taught Abraham how to heed God above all else. If you have heard God speak, and darkness follows, wait for the Father to direct you before you take the next step. Continue to work, without faltering, doing the normal duties that are part of the general will of God. Walk by faith, knowing that God is going to bring about what he has spoken to you. Do not dwell on your darkness so that you become discouraged and you waver in your absolute faith in God, listening instead to voices other than God. When his will comes about, in his time and in his way, your faith will have risen to a higher level of maturity, for you will have learned the peaceful contentment from heeding the voice of God.

4: DIVINE DARKNESS

"TURNING ALL OUR HOPE UPON GOD"

Divine Darkness: A state in which God places one in a period of extended, mostly private meditation for the purpose of producing deeper fellowship with God in order to reveal the powerful spiritual insights gleaned during this time.

The LORD is my rock and my fortress and my deliverer; the God of my strength, in whom I will trust; my shield and the horn of my salvation, my stronghold and my refuge; my Savior, You save me from violence. I will call upon the LORD, who is worthy to be praised; so shall I be saved from my enemies. (2 Sam. 22:2-4)

For You are my lamp, O LORD; the LORD shall enlighten my darkness. For by You I can run against a troop; by my God I can leap over a wall. As for God, His way is perfect; the word of the LORD is proven; He is a shield to all who trust in Him.
(2 Sam. 22:29-31)

The Lord lives! Blessed be my Rock! Let God be exalted, the Rock of my salvation! . . . I will give thanks to You, O Lord, . . . and sing praises to Your name.
(2 Sam. 22:47; 49-50)

This scripture passage contains the words of a song that David wrote after "the Lord delivered him from the hand of all his enemies, and from the hand of Saul" (2 Sam. 22:1). David was the one described by God as "a man after my own heart, who will do all my will" (Acts 13:22; also 1 Sam. 13:14).

Now he was not without faults and failures in his life. David is known for the sin of adultery that he committed with Bathsheba. He is also known for a census he ordered, which displeased God, because David put his faith in numbers, rather than in the Lord on that particular occasion. But both times, David acknowledged his sin (see 2 Sam. 12:13; 24:10), repented of his sins, and God knew that the repentance was sincere. God forgave David, but those particular sins did receive severe punishment (2 Sam. 12:14; 24:12-15), and the consequences of them caused problems again later in David's life.

The divine darkness that David experienced, though, was not punishment for sin, but it was divine discipline to mold David into a man after God's own heart, who would do all God's will. In the two previous chapters, two purposes for divine darkness have been examined: divine darkness trains us to hear God, and divine darkness teaches us to heed God. In this chapter, a third purpose for divine darkness will be addressed: *divine darkness turns all our hope upon God.*

> *The divine darkness that David experienced, though, was not punishment for sin, but it was divine discipline to mold David into a man after God's own heart, who would do all God's will.*

We have a tendency in our lives to get more self-sufficient when things are going our way. Isn't it a shame that during the good, smooth, pleasant times, we tend not to spend the time in communion and fellowship with God that we should? Our prayer times are shorter. Our Bible study is without the unction and urgency that we have when we are desperately seeking God's guidance. One reason God allows difficulties to come on us is to keep us dependent upon him and dedicated to his will for our lives. When we get self-sufficient, we leave God out of areas of our lives where he wants to work through us. The third purpose of divine darkness is to purge all self-sufficiency out of your life so that he will be your all-sufficiency. All your hope is turned completely upon God. Divine darkness has turned all your hope upon God when you rely upon the Lord, restrain through the Lord, and rejoice in the Lord.

Rely Upon the Lord

To turn all your hope upon God begins with *relying upon the Lord* absolutely and completely. In chapter two, reference was made to Isaiah 50:10. In the New King James Version of the Bible (NKJV), this verse is translated, "Who among you fears the LORD? Who obeys the voice of His Servant? Who walks in darkness And has no light? Let him trust in the name of the LORD and rely upon his God." The KJV uses "stay" instead of "rely" in its translation. But the meanings are the same. As was mentioned in chapter two, the picture is to "lean or support oneself on something." In divine darkness, you are to rely, to stay, and to lean on God alone. There are three reasons why you need to rely upon the Lord: for preservation, for provision, and for protection.

In the passage from 2 Samuel 22, David acknowledged that he relied upon God alone *for preservation* through the calamities of life. In 2 Samuel 22:19, David revealed that "the Lord was my stay." The Hebrew word, translated *support* or *stay* in verse 19, comes from the same root word in Hebrew as *stay* or *rely* in Isaiah 50:10 and *lean* in Proverbs 3:5. In the spiritual dark, you are to find support upon the "everlasting arms" (Deut. 33:27) of the Lord.

As you rely upon the Lord for your support in dark times, he will strengthen you. David expressed this fact which he knew from experience: "Oh, love the LORD, all you His saints! For the LORD preserves the faithful, and fully repays the proud person. Be of good courage, and He shall strengthen your heart, all you who hope in the LORD" (Ps. 31:23-24).

David acknowledged that God was his support, his strength, and his security: "The LORD is my rock and my fortress and my deliverer; the God of my strength, in whom I will trust; my shield and the horn of my salvation, my stronghold and my refuge; my Savior, You save me from violence" (2 Sam. 22:2-3). As his "rock" and his "stronghold," God was David's support. As his "shield," the "horn of my salvation," and the One in whom he could "trust," God was his strength. As David's "fortress," his "refuge," and his "Savior," God was his security. God was the one David completely relied upon for preservation.

The context of 2 Samuel 22:19 centers upon God delivering David from all his enemies. But from other writings of David, we know that he totally relied upon God in all facets of his life. *For the provisions* of life, David knew that there was no want to those who fear and trust God. "The Lord is my shepherd; I shall not want" were words he penned, knowing that God would provide for his every need just as a caring shepherd would look after his sheep. David trusted God to be his sustenance in the dark times he experienced: "The LORD knows the days of the upright, and their inheritance shall be forever. They shall not be ashamed in the evil time, and in the days of famine they shall be satisfied" (Psalm 37:18-19; 25). David knew that God would not forsake him, even in times of famine.

David knew that his supply for all his needs would come from God. When his fleeing from Saul first began, and he sought refuge before Abimelech, which also proved to be unsafe, David wrote, "Oh, taste and see that the LORD is good; blessed is the man who trusts in Him! Oh, fear the LORD, you His saints! There is no want to those who fear Him. The young lions lack and suffer hunger; but those who seek the LORD shall not lack any good thing"(Ps. 34:8-10).

We find the promise of God's provision for us confirmed in the New Testament. Jesus said, "But seek first the kingdom of God and His righteousness, and all these things shall be added to you" (Matt. 6:33). The Lord summarized in that one verse how God would provide our food and clothing. From a prison cell, the apostle Paul wrote, "And my God shall supply all your need according to His riches in glory by Christ Jesus" (Phil. 4:19). You can rely upon the Lord God for your provision during times of spiritual darkness.

David relied upon the Lord *for protection*. He knew that God was the one who would help him: "The LORD is my strength and my shield; my heart trusted in Him, and I am helped; therefore my heart greatly rejoices, and with my song I will praise Him. The LORD is their strength, and He is the saving refuge of His anointed" (Ps. 28:7-8). The protection of God was David's harbor of refuge through the good and the bad. He trusted God to care for him: "In You, O LORD, I put my trust; let me never be ashamed; deliver me in Your righteousness. Bow down Your ear to me, deliver me speedily; be my rock of refuge, a fortress of defense to save me. For You are my rock and my fortress; therefore, for Your name's sake, lead me and guide me" (Ps. 31:1-3). David testified to all who God was and that he was the one whom they could hold on to for protection at all times: "Cast your burden on the Lord, and He shall sustain you; He shall never permit the righteous to be moved" (Ps. 55:22).

In times of fear and frustration, David sought the Lord, and God delivered him from all his fears (Ps. 34:7), faults, and frustrations. God was the foundation and fortress David relied upon, especially during the years he experienced darkness. There are many other verses in the Bible from the writings of David that reinforce and testify to his absolute and complete reliance upon God. As he was nearing the end of his life, and he penned the words of 2 Samuel 22, David acknowledged that God had always seen him through the times of darkness, and therefore, all his hope was turned upon God.

Restrain Through the Lord

There is a second step by which divine darkness exercises you to turn all your hope upon God. As you have learned to completely rely upon the Lord, then you must *restrain yourself through the Lord*. In divine darkness, there is a period of staying and waiting upon the Lord until he brings you out of the spiritual dark. At this point, either you have still not heard the special word of God to you, or you have received his

> *You must keep from getting ahead of God because every time you do, it will eventually knock you backward several steps.*

message, but the time of making it known or its being fulfilled has not been granted. It can be very frustrating. You must keep from getting ahead of God because every time you do, it will eventually knock you backward several steps. Restraint is needed!

You do not want to make a move or speak a word without the approval of God because the Lord wants your obedience above all else (1 Sam. 15:22). If you try to get ahead of God, especially in the spiritual dark, it is like trying to walk through your own house at the darkest point of the night. You will bump into or knock over several things in your home that you can clearly see when it is light. Trying to walk in the darkness of your home, without turning on the lights, can result in your getting hurt, and it can also cause damage to some of your possessions. You can even be injured by things that are meant for your benefit and comfort, yet they can harm you in the dark when you cannot see them. When you try to walk ahead of God in divine darkness, it is going to do much more harm than any good which could be momentarily gained.

A specific reference is not made in the 2 Samuel 22 concerning waiting upon the Lord and restraining yourself through him. But it is sensed "between the lines" and within the words of this passage, when considering the life of David and his other writings. We learn from David three areas where restraint is needed during divine darkness. You must restrain your mouth, your mind, and your movements.

In Psalm 39:1-3, the Bible records these words of David: "I said, 'I will guard my ways, lest I sin with my tongue; I will restrain my mouth with a muzzle, while the wicked are before me.' I was mute with silence, I held my peace even from good; and my sorrow was stirred up. My heart was hot within me; while I was musing, the fire burned. Then I spoke with my tongue." Divine darkness is a time when it is best to *restrain your mouth*. You must be careful concerning what comes out of your mouth.

To restrain his mouth, David acknowledged that he had to guard his ways (Ps. 39:1). As David restrained his mouth by guarding his ways, the same is true for your life when you are in divine darkness. You need to guard your pathways. Be careful where you go and what you do because that has a great influence on what you say. David was careful to keep his steps within the pathways God had provided for him, even when they led him down paths with travel-impeding barriers. As a result, he could say, "I waited patiently for the LORD; and He inclined to me, and heard my cry. He also brought me up out of a horrible pit, out of the miry clay, and set my feet upon a rock, and established my steps. He has put a new song in my mouth—praise to our God; many will see it and fear, and will trust in the LORD" (Ps. 40:1-3). David restrained his mouth to cry only unto the Lord. God's pathway eventually put a new song of praise and joy upon his lips.

As you follow God's pathway, even in the case of David when it was fleeing for his life, you should go without panicking. Too many Christians blow a witness for Christ because they fall apart in the thick of a trial. The unsaved and the unchurched are not as greatly affected by our walk with the Lord during the smooth, easy, pleasant times than they are affected by our walk with the Lord during the rough, difficult, unpleasant times. They expect us to be full of joy, praise, and thanksgiving when everything is going our way. And we should be! But when our yoke is heavy to bear in life, we learn, as do others, just how genuine our walk of faith is in the Lord.

The unsaved, unchurched, and spiritually weak Christians are watching how you respond to adversity. When they see Christians remaining strong in the faith in the midst of difficult circumstances, they notice it. As you go about the duties of life during dark times, without panic, you become a light that reflects Christ to others. The light of Christ you reflect draws them to want what you have found in Jesus.

David restrained his mouth when he was in the spiritual dark. Much of the divine darkness that David experienced was while on the run or in dealing with his enemies. One of the most difficult things any of us ever has to face is in wanting to speak out in our defense when criticized or falsely accused. Psalm 62 and Psalm 63, both psalms of David, reveal how he dealt with his enemies and his critics. He said that he would wait silently on God alone to defend him and deliver him (Ps. 62:1-2, 5-8). David trusted God alone to stop the mouths of those who spoke lies against him (Ps. 63:11).

Divine darkness is a time to wait silently on God's defense so that you will not speak in a spirit of anger, frustration, and vengeance. But as you restrain your mouth in what you say to or before other people, it is a time to pour out your heart to God (Ps. 62:8). Follow the example of David in giving yourself to prayer (Ps. 109:4) in order to restrain your mouth. In the first four verses of Psalm 109, David poured his heart out to God concerning the lies and criticism others had spoken about him. But David resolved to give himself to prayer and meditation (Ps. 39:3) while trusting God to deal with his enemies. When the Lord let him know that it was time to speak, then he would speak.

David not only restrained his mouth while in divine darkness, but he *restrained his mind*. The key to restraining the mouth is in being careful in what you allow to influence your mind. David wanted his thoughts to be restrained within the limits of God's control, as he indicated in Psalm 19:14: "Let the words of my mouth and the meditation of my heart be acceptable in Your sight, O LORD, my strength and my Redeemer." The phrase, "the meditation of my heart," refers to the mind, emotions, and will.

It is important in restraining your mind to remove the waste that influences the mind negatively. Jesus said, "But those things which proceed out of the mouth come from the heart, and they defile a man. For out of the heart proceed evil thoughts, murders, adulteries, fornications, thefts, false witness, blasphemies" (Matt. 15:18-19). What you think about has a tremendous influence on your words and actions. The influences you expose your mind to produce your thoughts. So much conflict today is the result of people thinking about something that very often is just a rumor. Yet, if you dwell on it long enough, you will begin to believe something that most likely is not even a fact or the truth. This can result

> *You are what you think about most of the time.*

in friendships breaking up, and even churches experiencing conflict, because someone let their mind be influenced by unsubstantiated gossip, causing their thoughts to go haywire.

The Bible says that as you think in your heart, so are you (Prov. 23:7). You are what you think about most of the time. If you are not showing it now on the outside, eventually you will. When you are in divine darkness, be very careful what you allow to influence your mind. Take "every thought into captivity of the obedience of Christ" (2 Cor. 10:5). This is done by reflecting upon the Word of God.

David restrained his mouth and mind, while in divine darkness, by reflecting daily upon the scriptures. In divine darkness, you need to reflect upon the Word that indoctrinates the mind. To indoctrinate the mind through the scriptures is to get into the Word of God and to get the Word of God into you. David began and ended the day meditating upon God's Word and getting it indoctrinated into his heart. He wrote, "O God, You are my God; early will I seek You; . . . I meditate on You in the night watches. . . . You have been my help" (Ps. 63:1, 6-7). David also wrote, "I delight to do your will, O my God, and Your law is within my heart" (Ps. 40:8). David gave priority to meditating upon the Word of God (Ps. 119:97).

The reason God's law or God's Word was in David's heart was because he not only read the Word of God, but he got the Word of God into himself. Meditation was the way by which David got the Word within his heart. Meditation is more than reading, studying, and memorizing the scriptures. It is to go beyond that! It is to become so totally absorbed and saturated by a verse or a passage of the Bible so that you will think, act, react, and respond as God desires in the life application of those verses.

David also restrained his mind by remembering and reflecting upon the works of God which inspired him to continue to trust in God. In the difficulties of his life, David drew strength from how God had always taken care of him in the past. In Psalm 143:5-6 he said, "I remember the days of old; I meditate on all Your works; I muse on the work of Your hands. I spread out my hands to You; my soul longs for You like a thirsty land."

In divine darkness, you desperately long to hear from God. To keep restrained until God brings you out of the dark, you should remember his faithful and wondrous past works in your life and in the lives of others. One of the psalmists wrote, "I will remember the works of the LORD; surely I will remember Your wonders of old. I will also meditate on all Your work, and talk of Your deeds" (Ps. 77:11-12). In Psalm 119:15-16, 23-14, 27, which describes the benefits of meditating upon the Word of God, the writer expressed, "I will meditate on Your precepts, and contemplate Your ways. I will delight myself in Your statutes; I will not forget Your word. . . . Your servant meditates on Your statutes. Your testimonies also are my delight and my counselors. . . . Make me understand the way of Your precepts; so shall I meditate on Your wonderful works." If you are in the spiritual dark, then fill your mind with the completely faithful Word of God and the powerful, delivering works of God. Reflect upon his Word of promise and remember his works of past deliverance to help you restrain your mind.

David also learned to restrain his movements in divine darkness. Think about the difficulty of physically trying to do something or in trying to get someplace in the dark without the help of a light. You will probably make a total mess out of what you are trying to do, and you may end up far away from where you are trying to go. Divine darkness is a time spiritually to *restrain your movements* within the will of God.

In the previous chapter, it was mentioned that there are things you should continue to do in the general will of God when you are in divine darkness. You need to read the Bible daily, you should witness to the lost, you ought to encourage other Christians, and you need to be faithful to the worship services, programs, activities, and ministries of your church. But regarding personal decisions you are facing in your life, do not move too quickly.

You also need to *be cautious where you go*. The more difficult the situation may be, the greater you will have to fight the temptation to move ahead of God. As a young man, David had learned that he would be king of all Israel one day (1 Sam. 16:1, 12-13; 23:16-17). Yet he was on the run from King Saul for several years, even fearing for his life at times, before the will of God proved true in his life when he became king. Those years on the run were a time of darkness for David, yet they produced many of the most well-loved and favorite chapters, passages, and verses of the Bible. If he had not experienced divine darkness, we would not have had those psalms of David we find so comforting, encouraging, and uplifting.

David learned to restrain his movements in the darkness until God brought him out of the spiritual dark. David was later able to acknowledge, "He sent me from above, He took me, He drew me out of many waters. He delivered me from my strong enemy, . . . He also brought me out into a broad place; He delivered me because He delighted in me" (1 Sam. 22:17-18, 20). David turned all his hope upon God in divine darkness. In the worst of circumstances, he maintained a daily communion with God. He trusted God to show him where to go when it was time to move (Ps. 17:5), but he would not allow anything to move him, unless it was the will of God.

David also left us with an example of how we should confidently pray regarding the restraining of our movements during divine darkness. He said, "I have set the LORD always before me; because He is at my right hand I shall not be moved. Therefore my heart is glad, and my glory rejoices; my flesh also will rest in hope. . . . You will show me the path of life" (Ps. 16:8-9, 11). Actually, that is a prayer to pray regarding all of the situations of life. In divine darkness, ask God to show you his ways and to teach you his paths, but wait until he responds (Ps. 25:4-5). In his time, he will make your feet spiritually as sure and swift as a deer, and he will set you spiritually secure upon high places (2 Sam. 22:33-34).

You have reached a level spiritually of turning all your hope upon God when, in the spiritual dark, you restrain your mouth, your mind, and your movements, as you rely upon God to meet your every need. That is where God wants us to be all the time. But it sometimes takes a season of divine darkness to get us there or to get us back to such a level of trust and devotion to the Lord.

If you are in divine darkness today, the time and place you are ready to be brought out of the darkness is when you have no one you completely hope in other than God. God may wait longer before bringing you out of divine darkness, but when he does, you will confidently know from experience this prayer of David:

> *I waited patiently for the LORD; and He inclined to me, and heard my cry. He also brought me up out of a horrible pit, out of the miry clay, and set my feet upon a rock, and established my steps. He has put a new song in my mouth—praise to our God; many will see it and fear, and will trust in the LORD. Blessed is that man who makes the LORD his trust, and does not respect the proud, nor such as turn aside to lies. (Ps. 40:1-4)*

The new song that God will put in your mouth will be a message to speak in the light for others to hear. It will be an effective message because your example will back up your words. You will have learned to restrain yourself in the Lord by completely trusting in God and depending upon him to bring you out of the darkness. As a result, your walk of faith will move to a higher level of sacrifice, satisfaction, security, service, and stability.

Rejoice In The Lord

The final step that gives evidence you have been exercised and trained by divine darkness is when you have reached a spiritual level of faith where you *rejoice in the Lord*, not only because of deliverance from darkness, but even while you are in the depths of darkness. Second Samuel 22:1 states, "Then David spoke to the LORD the words of this song, on the day when the

LORD had delivered him from the hand of all his enemies, and from the hand of Saul." This song was a way by which David rejoiced in the Lord because of his deliverance by God. Here are some examples of his rejoicing in the Lord:

> *I will call upon the Lord, who is worthy to be praised; so shall I be saved from my enemies (2 Sam. 22:4).*

> *The Lord lives! Blessed be my Rock! Let God be exalted, the Rock of my salvation! (2 Sam. 22:47)*

> *He delivers me from my enemies. You also lift me up above those who rise against me; You have delivered me from the violent man. Therefore I will give thanks to You, O LORD, among the Gentiles, and sing praises to Your name. (2 Sam. 22:49-50)*

We also know from the psalms of David, many of which were birthed while he was in spiritual darkness, that he rejoiced in the Lord, even when in the midst of great distress before deliverance had come.

As we look at rejoicing in the Lord as part of the process of turning all our hope upon God, the word *rejoice* will be used to describe what is also referred to in the Bible as "praise" and "thanksgiving." Different Hebrew and Greek words are used for *rejoice*, *praise*, and *thanksgiving*, but they are all connected in their application in and to our lives. In 2 Samuel 22:50, David said, "I will give thanks to you, O Lord, . . . and sing praises to Your name." In Psalm 33:1, the Bible says, "Rejoice in the Lord, O you righteous! For praise from the upright is beautiful." Psalm 97:12 says, "Rejoice in the Lord, you righteous, and give thanks at the remembrance of His holy name." Those verses show how the words, *rejoice*, *praise*, and *thanksgiving*, are used interchangeably and cooperatively with one another in the Bible.

From the life of David, and from the whole counsel of the Bible, we learn three reasons why we ought to rejoice in the Lord, even while in divine darkness: because of expectation, in anticipation, and in appreciation.

A first reason why we ought to rejoice in the Lord, regardless of our circumstances, is *because God expects us to.* But it is not because of its benefit to God, or that he cannot bless us or acknowledge his love for us if we do not praise him. The Old Testament reveals to us how God would bless his people abundantly, but eventually, they would depend less and less on God, even turning from him. But he still showed love and forgiveness with them because his love is everlasting (Jer. 31:3).

Rejoicing in the Lord is for our benefit. To express our joy, praise, and thanksgiving to God will uplift us and renew our hope, even in the midst of divine darkness. What are some of the reasons for which we can rejoice when we are in spiritual darkness? We can be thankful to God for our salvation, the scriptures, security, sustenance, the Holy Spirit, and soundness of mind, soul, and body. It is amazing what praising can do! Make it a habit to "praise the LORD! For it is good to sing praises to our God; for it is pleasant, and praise is beautiful" (Ps. 147:1). If things are so dark for you that you do not feel there is anything for which you can rejoice, then "rejoice

> *The Lord sees you in your darkness and he is your way out of darkness.*

in hope of the glory of God" (Rom. 5:2). The Lord sees you in your darkness and he is your way out of darkness. As you turn all your hope upon God, you can be assured that "hope does not disappoint" (Rom. 5:5).

It is also for our best to rejoice in the Lord because God expects us to. The apostle Paul stated, "In everything give thanks; for this is the will of God in Christ Jesus for you" (1 Thess. 5:18). It is for our best to do what is the will of God for us. To give thanks is to be the norm for the Christian. Paul does not mean that we should thank God for everything we encounter. Some of the things we encounter are certainly not of God, but they are allowed by God. We should not rejoice and be thankful for things that dishonor God. But we can be thankful in everything. When we are affected by evil, we can still be thankful for who God is, for his presence, for the good he can bring even through that which is bad, because all things work together for good to them that love God (Rom. 8:28). We should be thankful in every situation and circumstance, even in adversity, as well as in prosperity.

It is also for others' benefit for us to rejoice in the Lord. Paul lived a life of rejoicing and thanksgiving whether he was in a prison or a palace, in adversity or prosperity, or in poor health or good health. An incident that occurred in the life of Paul, when he first established his ministry for Christ in Philippi, is recorded in Acts 16. After Paul and his companion, Silas, were beaten severely and imprisoned for preaching in the name of Jesus, the Bible says, "And at midnight Paul and Silas prayed, and sang praises unto God; and the prisoners heard them" (Acts 16:25 KJV). Paul and Silas turned a dark, gloomy prison into a glorious palace of praise. As they praised the Lord, he provided deliverance for them, and in the process, the jailer and his family were saved.

During a later imprisonment, Paul wrote to the church which he helped to establish at Philippi under such adverse conditions, to "rejoice in the Lord always. Again I will say, rejoice!" (Phil. 4:4). Those words were an encouragement and challenge to the believers at Philippi because they saw those words lived out in the life of the one who inspired Paul to write those words.

You can also *rejoice in anticipation of God's deliverance* when you are in divine darkness. As you sit in darkness, the Lord will be a light to you (Mic. 7:8). Let us be reminded again how Jeremiah anticipated the Lord's deliverance from his season of divine darkness. He said, "The LORD is good to those who wait for Him, to the soul who seeks Him. It is good that one should hope and wait quietly for the salvation of the LORD" (Lam. 3:25-26). If you are in divine darkness, deliverance will come, and when it does, it is a time to "arise, shine; for your light has come! And the glory of the LORD is risen upon you. For behold, the darkness shall cover the earth, and deep darkness the people; but the LORD will arise over you, and His glory will be seen upon you" (Isa. 60:1-2). As God brings light to your darkness, it will be of benefit to others, especially if God's message to you is what they need to get out of darkness too.

From his previous experiences, David knew that God would deliver him in time. Second Samuel 22:47-50 is an expression of thanksgiving to God after the Lord had delivered David from divine darkness. David, though, often expressed joy for God's deliverance long before it took place. David went from one trial to another for many years of his life. Yet, as God delivered him and took care of him in the midst of dark days, David learned to rejoice in the Lord in the

As God delivered him and took care of him in the midst of dark days, David learned to rejoice in the Lord in the worst of circumstances.

worst of circumstances. He anticipated the deliverance he knew God would eventually provide. Psalm 71 is among the psalms where David turned all his hope upon God, as he rejoiced in the Lord, knowing that God would see him through. This psalm was written in a time of great darkness and distress. God's deliverance had not yet come, but David anticipated that the Lord would take care of him. David wrote,

In You, O LORD, I put my trust; let me never be put to shame. Deliver me in Your righteousness, and cause me to escape; . . . For You are my hope, O Lord GOD; . . . My praise shall be continually of You. I have become as a wonder to many, But You are my strong refuge. Let my mouth be filled with Your praise And with Your glory all the day. . . . I will hope continually, and will praise You yet more and more. . . . You, who have shown me great and severe troubles, shall revive me again, and bring me up again from the depths of the earth. . . . I will praise You— and Your faithfulness, O my God! (Ps. 71:1-2, 5-8, 14, 20, 22)

David acknowledged (Ps. 71:20) that God allowed this darkness to come upon him, but he knew that God had a purpose in doing so and that God would bring him out of the darkness. By positive expression, David rejoiced in the Lord in anticipation of the deliverance of God. He knew from previous experiences that God's deliverance would come.

David composed so many of his psalms while experiencing great difficulties, but he was positive and upbeat as he reflected upon God's faithfulness to always see him through the dark times. He is a proven example for us how you should rejoice in anticipations of God's deliverance from divine darkness. In the two previous chapters, as we have learned from the lives of Job, Abraham, and Jeremiah, we have seen proven examples how *the God who disciplines us through divine darkness will also deliver us from it.*

If you are in divine darkness, and you have not yet rejoiced in the Lord, then do so! It is amazing what praising can do! You have proven examples from the Bible and in the lives of people all around you who have experienced divine darkness too. The Lord's compassion, mercies, and faithfulness are great. They never fail (Lam. 3:22-23)! From your own previous experiences and through the proven examples of others, you have a reason to express positively your joy in the Lord, if you are in divine darkness. His deliverance will come.

There is a third reason why you ought to rejoice in the Lord because of divine darkness. You should *rejoice in appreciation for God's deliverance from darkness*. It occurs after the Lord has brought you out of divine darkness, and it is your thanks-offering to God. Second Samuel 22 is a thanks-offering David gave to God, in the form of a song, in appreciation for God's liberation. In this song of praise, he described the distress that he had experienced and how God had delivered him from his enemies (2 Sam. 22:1, 4, 18, 49). He also described how God had delivered him from the strivings (contentions) of the people David ruled (2 Sam. 22:44). He had been liberated from spiritual darkness, and David expressed his appreciation to God privately and publicly through singing praises to his name (2 Sam. 22:50). David knew the importance of rejoicing in the Lord. When the ark of God was returned to Jerusalem, after the Philistines had captured it (1 Sam. 4:17) and then returned it across the border, where it had remained in the house of Abinadab, in Kirjath Jearim (1 Sam. 7:1), David privately penned a song of thanksgiving (1 Chron. 16:7-36). It became a public song of praise (1 Chron. 16:7). He appointed "Levites to minister before the ark of the Lord to commemorate, to thank, and praise the Lord God of Israel" (1 Chron. 16:4). As Asaph led the singers to perform the song, when it had ended, "all the people said, 'Amen!' and praised the Lord" (1 Chron. 16:36). David knew that it was important for the people he led to also rejoice in the Lord. His song of appreciation led the people to rejoice in the Lord by their remembering God's marvelous works, wonders, and Word (1 Chron. 16:12, 15), and by their reflecting that remembrance in verbal witnessing about God's salvation through a visible worship which showed their thanks.

From this particular occasion in the life of David, we see praise elevated to its highest expression in thanks being made to God—in this instance, for the liberation of the Ark of the Covenant—but the praise was rooted in those times of darkness and despair, when David learned the importance of praising God anyhow. David pled with God on one occasion to "bring my soul out of prison, that I may praise Your name" (Ps. 42:7). David was referring to the prison of darkness. From his writings, including the text in 2 Samuel 22, we know that David lived up to his promise to praise God. He learned the importance of praising God, even in the midst of darkness. It helped to make rejoicing more exhilarating, sincere, and meaningful when liberation and deliverance did come.

When we express our thanks and gratefulness to the Lord, there is an effect upon our lives that lifts our spirits. When we will just learn to thank God for life—for if you are presently in divine darkness, God still has you alive for a good reason—your showing appreciation to God can lead to greater personal benefits.

In the seventeenth chapter of Luke, an account is given of Christ healing ten lepers. When they asked Jesus to have mercy on them (Luke 17:13), he said, "Go, show yourselves to the priests" (Luke 17:14). According to their law, a person cured of leprosy had to be declared clean of the disease by a priest (Lev. 14:2) before he could once again get out and live a normal life in

> *When we express our thanks and gratefulness to the Lord, there is an effect upon our lives that lifts our spirits.*

society. The ten lepers did respond in faith to what the Lord had asked them to do, and the Bible says, "And so it was that as they went, they were cleansed" (Luke 17:14). Yet only one of the lepers returned to give thanks to Jesus for restoration to a healthy life. Luke 17:15 says, "With a loud voice" the leper "glorified God." This healed leper praised the Lord in appreciation for deliverance from the most dreaded disease of that day.

The appreciation of this healed leper touched the Lord. Jesus made those around him aware that only one of the ten healed lepers returned "to give glory to God" (Luke 17:17). Our Lord had another blessing to give those he had healed—a greater blessing than healthy life—but only one returned to receive it. All of the lepers had received a healthier life, but the grateful leper also received the gift of heavenly life.

There was something that those ten lepers needed that was even greater than being healed of a horrible disease. The priest could declare them cleansed and delivered from sin. Only one of the lepers received the greater healing, the greater blessing, the greater gift—eternal life through Jesus Christ our Lord. The one leper offered thanks in appreciation to the one who delivered him from the dark, disabling effects of a dreadful disease, but the greater blessing is that he received deliverance from the dark, deadly effects of sin. You should also rejoice in appreciation of God's deliverance from divine darkness, not only for your liberation and the fresh life restored to you, but also for the spiritual light that has resulted and that radiates within you and from you.

A grateful heart has a positive effect outwardly on others, but its most positive effect is what it does for you inwardly and personally. If you do not express thanks to someone who has helped to deliver you from a difficult situation, you might find yourself dwelling on why you had to experience the adversity in the first place. That can lead to bitterness. If you will rejoice in the Lord, especially when the Lord has delivered you out of divine darkness, it will lead you to focus your attention off the pain and hurt of dark times onto the one who brought you out of it. Instead of the experience making you bitter, it makes you better. Thus, the divine darkness has exercised and trained you for God's intended purpose.

> *A grateful heart has a positive effect outwardly on others, but its most positive effect is what it does for you inwardly and personally.*

Divine darkness turns all our hope upon God. It leaves you with nowhere else to turn and with no one else to trust in but God alone. That is the place at which God can accomplish the most through you. "For it is God who works in you both to will and to do for His good pleasure" (Phil. 2:13). That is how he has chosen to reveal himself to this world—through us. May we shine outwardly as the apostle Paul challenged us: "Do all things without complaining and disputing, that you may become blameless and harmless, children of God without fault in the midst of a crooked and perverse generation, among whom you shine as lights in the world"

(Phil. 2:14-15). When God brings you out of spiritual darkness back into the light, the glow of Christ will radiate from you, if you respond in joy and gratefulness to what God has intended to produce in you through divine darkness.

CONCLUSION

David relied completely on God when he was in divine darkness. He restrained himself through the Lord to keep from thinking, speaking, or moving out of the will of God. He exemplified a life that rejoiced in the Lord, in times of difficulty and after deliverance had come. David was a man after God's own heart because his faith, trust, and hope were in God alone. Oh, he made mistakes—some very big ones. There were times in his life when he acted in self-sufficiency, instead of in the all-sufficiency of God. David had to suffer God's punishment and correction on those occasions. Yet he acknowledged his sin, confessed, repented, and God forgave him. David knew he got what he deserved, and he also knew that he sometimes did not get what he really deserved for his disobedience to God. But David allowed God's divine discipline to bend him, break him, melt him, and mold him, whether it was punishment because of his straying from God's will or it was for the purpose of moving him to a higher level of faith and maturity in God's will.

You may be in divine darkness right now, even though you have heard God's voice and you have heeded what he has spoken to you. If so, then turn all your hope upon God. Rely upon God for preservation, provision, protection, and power in the daily concerns of life. Restrain your mouth, your mind, and your movements through the help and strength of the Lord. Rejoice in the Lord out of expectation, anticipation, and appreciation for his deliverance. It will come, for "the word of the Lord is proven" (2 Sam. 22:31).

Turn all your hope upon God. God and God alone is your lamp, enlightening your darkness (2 Sam. 22:29) through the providential guidance of his perfect way for your life (2 Sam. 22:31), and through the revelation and confirmation in his proven Word, as it relates to the circumstances of your life.

5: DIVINE DARKNESS

"THE TREASURES OF DARKNESS"

Divine Darkness: A state in which God places one in a period of extended, mostly private meditation for the purpose of producing deeper fellowship with God in order to reveal the powerful spiritual insights gleaned during this time.

I will go before you and make the crooked places straight; I will break in pieces the gates of bronze and cut the bars of iron. I will give you the treasures of darkness and hidden riches of secret places, that you may know that I, the LORD, Who call you by your name, am the God of Israel. (Isa. 45:2-3)

Three chapters have already been devoted to the divine discipline of darkness. Most of you are probably ready to get out of darkness and on to something else. But there is the necessity to address one more chapter on the subject of divine darkness. This chapter will not be as extensive and detailed as the three previous chapters, but it will be more like a "p.s." that we sometimes add at the end of a letter when there is something else that we just have to say.

Until I began to read the thoughts of Oswald Chambers concerning the divine discipline of darkness, and until I heard evangelist Bill Stafford preach a sermon in 1987 that dealt with this topic, I had always thought of spiritual darkness in its negative and evil sense. Among the most popular Christian books in recent times have been fictional books with stories based on the evil powers of darkness and the spiritual warfare in which Christians are engaged. That was the way I had basically viewed the concept of darkness from a biblical and spiritual perspective. It was a justified view. There are dark, evil forces in the unseen world, as well as in the seen world, which Christians must be prepared to deal with. Chapter seven will give some space to that subject.

There is also, though, a positive, good darkness that is a justified view, biblically and spiritually, because this divine darkness comes from the Lord God. The three previous chapters have dealt extensively with the purposes of divine darkness. We have seen how Job, Abraham, Jeremiah, and David were divinely disciplined by divine darkness. We know that Isaiah (see Isa. 45:3, 7; 50:10) and Micah (see Mic. 7:8) were knowledgeable of divine darkness and knew how to respond to it. Most likely, they had also been divinely exercised by it. All six of those men were trained by divine darkness to greater spiritual fitness and to higher levels of faith. It made them greater men of God. If divine darkness has come upon your life, it is meant to make you a greater servant of the Lord.

As has been previously mentioned, divine darkness is a very tough discipline to endure. It is probably the hardest spiritually of all the divine disciplines, although they are all tough in their own respective ways. One reason why divine darkness is so hard to experience is because many Christians are unaware of it, just like I was for many years of my Christian life. In coming to a knowledge of this divine discipline of God, I now see how God used this discipline in the lives of many of our modern day heroes of the Christian faith, as well as in the lives of the examples we have seen in the Bible. As I have read the life stories, and as I continue to read about spiritual giants of past years and this present day, nearly

> *As I continue to read about spiritual giants of past years and this present day, nearly all of them have experienced times of divine darkness.*

all of them have experienced times of divine darkness. Some of the times of divine darkness occurred after they were already looked upon and respected as great spiritual leaders. The divine darkness came about to make them even greater men and women of God.

THE TREASURES OF DARKNESS

What is the "p.s." that just has to be said at the end of this study of divine darkness? Isaiah 45:3 contains the message that needs to be left with us as we close our look at the divine discipline of darkness. The Lord speaks through the prophet Isaiah in this verse, and this is his message to us: "I will give you the treasures of darkness and hidden riches of secret places." There are *treasures of darkness* and hidden riches you may never find unless you experience divine darkness.

How many movies, books, and stories have centered a plot around finding a hidden treasure? There are scores of them, and how thrilling and exciting it is when the hidden treasure is found by the heroes of the story. Most of the time, they have to go through disappointments and difficulties before they finally find the treasure. It is the same way with divine darkness. There are treasures of darkness, but the road to them can be very difficult—so difficult, at times, that you want to give up trying to find the hidden treasures, and you just want the Lord to get you out of the darkness.

What are the treasures of darkness? Three chapters have already been devoted to the purposes for which God brought divine darkness upon the lives of three Bible personalities: to train us to *hear* God (Job); to teach us to *heed* God (Abraham); and to turn all our *hope* upon God (David). Those are reasons why God brings divine darkness upon our lives. For each of those reasons, we learned specific ways for what must be done in a person's life to be exercised and trained by divine darkness.

To give you a glimpse of just some of the treasures of darkness, this study will be limited to the text in Isaiah 45:2-3. To some degree, learning to hear God, to heed God, and to hope in God are treasures of darkness in themselves. But the real treasures of darkness are the discovering and the possessing of principles and truths of God that will not only benefit you in hearing, heeding, and hoping in God, but they will benefit you in all areas of your walk of faith.

PROPHESIED ABOUT A HEATHEN KING

Before we go through Isaiah 45:2-3 phrase by phrase to get a look at the treasures of darkness, let us get the background on the historical significance of this passage. These two verses are prophecies Isaiah made concerning Cyrus (see Isa. 44:28; 45:1), the king of Persia, about two centuries before the birth of Cyrus. One reason why God made this prophecy through Isaiah was to give credibility to the prophecies he had already made concerning the birth of Christ (Isa. 7:14), which would occur about seven hundred years later. It was also to give credibility to the purpose for which Jesus would come to earth (Isa. 9:6-7). Isaiah also prophesied in greater detail about the coming Messiah a few chapters later in the book of Isaiah.

The literal fulfillment of the prophecy in Isaiah 45:2-3 occurred when Cyrus became king of Persia. God used this heathen Gentile king to allow the exiled Israelites to return back to their homeland (Ezra 1:1-4). When the Babylonians conquered the Southern Kingdom of Israel (Judah), they exiled the Jews from their land. The Babylonians had amassed great wealth through the nations they conquered. When Persia became the ruling world power under the reign of Cyrus, "the treasures of darkness and hidden riches of secret places" were the vast horde of material riches the Babylonians kept locked away in storage vaults. Those riches became the spoils of war for the Persians.

Nearly all Bible commentators see the passage in Isaiah 45 only in its historical significance. But there is a spiritual message in Isaiah 45:2-3 that goes beyond its literal sense. The "treasures of darkness and hidden riches of secret places" is a phrase containing words that are used elsewhere in the Bible to describe things other than material wealth. There are spiritual treasures of darkness and spiritual hidden riches found in secret places. Let us examine some of these in the light of Isaiah 45:2-3.

GOD'S PERPETUAL PRESENCE

I will go before you. (Isa. 45:2)

It was prophesied by Isaiah that God would go before Cyrus to smooth the way before him (Isa. 45:2). God would be with Cyrus to direct him and to give him victory over his foes. The Lord used this Gentile king of a heathen nation to defeat the Babylonians so that the Jews could return back to their homeland from exile. I believe that Cyrus came to be a believer in the one, true, living God (see 2 Chron. 36:22-23; Ezra 1:1-4), but there are many Bible commentators who would strongly disagree with me. Whether he was a monotheistic believer in God or not, we do know that God's presence was with Cyrus so that he would perform all God's pleasure (Isa. 44:22). Even if Cyrus was not a true believer in God, he was still greatly used by the Lord. Long before Cyrus was born, and the prophecy concerning him was to occur, he was promised the presence of God to go before him, to make his battles victorious, in order to fulfill the plan of God.

Now if God *promised his presence* to direct a heathen nation to world supremacy, you can be sure that God more strongly desires his presence in your life to accomplish his will. "It is God who works in you both to will and to do for His good pleasure" (Phil. 2:13). Paul was speaking to Christians in that verse. God said of Cyrus, "He is my shepherd, and he shall perform all My pleasure" (Isa. 44:28). The Lord would rather work through his own people to *perform his pleasure*, but sometimes we are not sensitive or obedient to his will, so he has to use someone other than his own people. Often in the Old Testament, we read how God used non-believers to punish and to get the attention of his people. But he also used them, such as with Cyrus, to rescue and to deliver his people.

It takes a man and woman after God's own heart, who will do all his will (Acts 13:22; 1 Sam. 13:14), to do his good pleasure. If we keep his commandments, we please him (1 John 3:22). Paul exhorted us to please God because we have been approved by God to speak for him, but he will test our hearts (1 Thess. 2:4). Divine darkness is a way by which God tests us. Job referred to his time of divine darkness as testing: "He knows the way that I take; when He has tested me, I shall come forth as gold" (Job 23:10). Remember, this was during a period of his life when Job did not feel like God's presence was with him. He longed to hear from God. It was a frustrating time. What did he do in the darkness? He sought God's voice and he stayed upon God until he heard the voice of God. Although he did not feel like the presence of God was with him, Job did believe God would perform what was appointed for him (Job 23:14). Job knew that God had allowed the darkness to come upon him, and even though he wondered if God would ever bring him out of it while he was on earth, he resolved to do what was right: "My foot has held fast to

His steps; I have kept His way and not turned aside. I have not departed from the commandment of His lips; I have treasured the words of His mouth more than my necessary food" (Job 23:11-12).

Job learned to treasure the presence of God in his life and upon his life more than anything else. From a man who had the greatest fame and fortune of anyone in his part of the world, the greatest treasure of darkness that Job found was to hear from God and to have the *perpetual presence* of God in his life.

In divine darkness, you know God is there, but you feel like he is not there. You call upon him and seek him, but you just cannot seem to find his will and direction for your life. It gets you to the point where you desperately want to clearly hear God's voice again and clearly see the light of his presence in your life. You realize that what matters the most in your walk of faith is just that. When you stay true to God in the spiritual darkness, then when he brings you out of it, it confirms that God has been with you all the time as the process has spiritually matured you. God's presence is perpetual. He is there with us in the dark times, although we really wonder if he is. He is allowing those dark times to melt us, mold us, and make us better.

Sometimes, God's presence is more *visible and vocal* to us than at other times, but he is always there. As Moses encouraged Joshua, when Joshua was chosen as the successor of Moses, those words, which are confirmed again and again throughout the Bible, are applicable to us today: "And the LORD, He is the one who goes before you. He will be with you, He will not leave you nor forsake you; do not fear nor be dismayed" (Deut. 31:8). *God's perpetual presence* is with us. As you come through divine darkness, relying upon the Lord and waiting for him, you exhibit faith in God. This pleases him (Heb. 11:6). Your faith in God grows stronger (1 Thess. 4:1). You know that whether things are good or bad, God's perpetual presence will *sustain you* (Prov. 3:5; 55:22) *and satisfy you* as he uses you to perform his pleasure and to reveal his eternal presence for all who will receive his gift of eternal life through Jesus Christ.

GOD'S PREVAILING POWER

...and make the crooked places straight; I will break in pieces the gates of bronze and cut the bars of iron. (Isa. 45:2)

The Lord not only indicated that his presence would be with Cyrus to direct him, But *God's prevailing power* would bring defeat to the enemies of Cyrus and the Persians. God said that he would make the way smooth so that Cyrus and his army would march triumphantly right to the center of rule in the nations they fought. God said, "I will break in pieces the gates of bronze and cut the bars of iron" (Isa. 45:2). The cities during the time of Cyrus were protected by what appeared in some cities to be impenetrable walls and gates. Babylon was said to have gates of solid bronze. Historians differ as to whether they were really bronze or bronze-plated. Nevertheless, they looked impenetrable. But the Persian army penetrated into the city to defeat the Babylonians. Their strategy involved sneaking into the city through a dry river bed, then opening the gates from the controls that were inside the city walls.

Like the walls coming down at Jericho, God could have worked the same way at Babylon. But whether God displays his power through the *working of miracles* or by the *wisdom of mind* (the Persian strategy at Babylon) he gives to us, his desires will prevail. The Lord

> *In our lives, the evidence of the power of God upon us is not always so clear cut.*

prophesied through Isaiah that Cyrus would defeat those who had exiled the Israelites, and he provided his presence and power to lead the Persians to victory.

In our lives, the evidence of the power of God upon us is not always so clear cut. God manifests his power in our lives, not through our strengths, but through our weaknesses. That is contrary to human logic. But Paul acknowledged the Lord works that way so "that your faith should not be in the wisdom of men but in the power of God" (1 Cor. 2:5). Paul pleaded with God three different times to remove what he described as a "thorn in the flesh" (2 Cor. 12:7-8). The Lord told Paul, "My grace is sufficient for you, for my strength is made perfect in weakness" (2 Cor. 12:9). Paul's outlook toward whatever divine discipline brought upon him, or whatever the circumstances of life sent, was this: "Therefore most gladly I will rather boast in my infirmities, that the power of Christ may rest upon me. Therefore I take pleasure in infirmities, in reproaches, in needs, in persecutions, in distresses, for Christ's sake. For when I am weak, then I am strong" (2 Cor. 12:9-10).

Divine darkness is a time when outward signs point to your being at your weakest in many ways. And you feel weak! In divine darkness, Job had just about lost everything—his possessions, his children, his health, his power. But God's prevailing power was with him. As his power diminished, God's power was demonstrated. As a result, a physically, mentally, and spiritually broken man became a physically, mentally, and spiritually greater man. Job found treasures in the darkness—unswaying faith and trust in the perpetual presence of God and the prevailing power of God.

David found the same strength and power (2 Sam. 22:33) when he was at his weakest—in those times of darkness. He knew divine darkness was a place of God's prevailing power. When God enlightened his darkness, with the prevailing power of God upon him, David said, "For by You I can run against a troop; by my God I can leap over a wall. As for God, His way is perfect; the word of the LORD is proven; He is a shield to all who trust in Him" (2 Sam. 22:29-31). David turned all his hope upon God when he was in divine darkness. The expressions of his trust in God, many of which are recorded in the Bible, are spiritual treasures for us today. His darkness became our treasure.

Divine darkness drains you of all self-sufficiency. If you allow it to exercise you, it fills you with God's all-sufficiency. That is when the prevailing power of God is most realized in your life. It is when you are at your weakest that the greatest power of God is upon you. It is in darkness when you receive the greatest benefit from God's light. One of the treasures of darkness is discovering that "we have this treasure in earthen vessels, that the excellence of the power may be of God and not of us. We are hard pressed on every side, yet not crushed; we are perplexed, but not in despair; persecuted, but not forsaken; struck down, but not destroyed—always carrying about in the body the dying of the Lord Jesus, that the life of Jesus also may be manifested in our body" (2 Cor. 4:7-10). There is untapped power in your life that

> *There is untapped power in your life that you will never discover until you are completely depleted of your own power supply.*

you will never discover until you are completely depleted of your own power supply. It is like an emergency back-up system. You will never tap into this reserve until you are in extreme difficulty. But when you realize it is available, from your personal use of it, it becomes your treasure of darkness. You know where to find it when you need it, and you know that it is a power that will always prevail in its time.

PERSEVERING PRAYER

...and hidden riches of secret places. (Isa. 45:3)

As God's presence and power were with Cyrus and the Persian army to lead them to victory, their spoils of war included the treasuries of the nations they conquered. When Babylon fell to the Persians, the rich treasures the kings of Babylon had taken as their spoils of war became the treasures and riches of Cyrus. The riches of Jerusalem, especially the articles of the temple, had been removed when the Babylonians conquered Judah and exiled the Jews from their homeland. When the Persians gained control, Cyrus was stirred by the Lord to rebuild the temple, and he allowed the Jews to return to their homeland after seventy years of exile. He also brought out the silver and gold articles of the "house of the Lord," which Nebuchadnezzar had taken from Jerusalem, and he gave them back to the Jews to use again in their worship at the temple (see Ezra 1:1-11).

The Babylonians, in particular, had accumulated such great riches that much of it was locked up and stored away in vaults and storage chambers. Most of these riches were hidden away from sight, except from those who watched over them and guarded them. Cyrus allowed these treasures and hidden riches to be brought out from the dark and secret places where they were stored, especially the gold and silver articles that had been made for use in worship at the temple in Jerusalem. Isaiah 45:3 uses figurative language to describe what literally became true in material prosperity. But divine darkness is a place where you also find spiritual hidden riches of secret places.

As divine darkness comes into your life to train you to hear God, to teach you to heed God, and to turn all your hope upon God, it is a place where you pray like you have never prayed before, that is, if you allow this divine discipline to exercise you. You have got to keep from giving up in divine darkness. It is a time when you spend a lot of time talking to God and even crying before God. You feel as though he is not hearing you, but he is. As you continue in prayer, seeking to hear from God, when the time is right, you will get your word from God. In getting that word from God, you have learned what it is to persevere in prayer.

Persevering prayer is a treasure of divine darkness. That is the spiritual significance of the phrase, "the hidden riches of secret places." There is a truth and principle in this verse that goes beyond its literal, historical significance. When Jesus was teaching about prayer, he said, "But you, when you pray, go into your room, and when you have shut your door, pray to your Father who is in the secret place; and your Father who sees in secret will reward you openly" (Matt. 6:6).

Daniel knew how to persevere in prayer in his secret place, and he knew the hidden riches of secret places. He had been exiled after the Babylonian takeover of Judah. He was chosen, along with three of his Hebrew friends, Shadrach, Meshach, and Abed-Nego, to serve in King Nebuchadnezzar's palace. When the king asked his wise men (special advisors who basically made use of magic, astrology, and sorcery) to do what even they said was impossible for man (Dan. 2:10-11)—interpret a dream without knowing its content—Daniel was able to do it. He asked his three friends to pray for God's mercy concerning the dream, then he went to his "prayer closet," his secret place, to pray it through. The king's dream was revealed to Daniel by God (Dan. 2:19, 28), and he was able to give its interpretation. As a result, the king made Daniel ruler over the whole province of Babylon, and he was also made chief over all the wise men of Babylon (Dan. 2:48).

Even during dark times—a time of exile for the Jews—God worked on behalf of those who stayed true to him and who completely trusted in him. Daniel said,

> *Blessed be the name of God forever and ever, for wisdom and might are His. And He changes the times and the seasons; He removes kings and raises up kings; He gives wisdom to the wise and knowledge to those who have understanding. He reveals deep and secret things; He knows what is in the darkness, and light dwells with Him.* (Dan. 2:20-22)

Daniel was "rewarded openly" (Matt. 6:6) with a position of prominence and prestige which was materially beneficial to him. But Daniel discovered hidden riches of secret places that had far more value than a monetary price. He was known for his wisdom, knowledge, and as one "in whom is the Spirit of the Holy God" (Dan. 5:11-12). Daniel learned, as Isaiah personally learned and expressed so well, "Wisdom and knowledge will be the stability of your times, and the strength of salvation; the fear of the LORD is His treasure" (Isa. 33:6). God's wisdom, knowledge, and salvation are the stability of our times and our treasure. The Bible says in Proverbs 2:4 to search for wisdom as for hidden treasures. The fear of the Lord is the beginning of knowledge (Prov. 1:7), and that is how wisdom and knowledge from God increase (Prov. 2:5-7). To fear the Lord is to have faith, trust, and respect in him and to show it in *submissiveness* to his Word and to his will (Prov. 2:1). As a time of divine discipline in the life of Daniel will be examined in chapter seven, we will see that he was one who feared the Lord.

> *In the secret place of prayer, Daniel found the wisdom and knowledge of God which became his stability during dark and difficult days.*

In the secret place of prayer, Daniel found the wisdom and knowledge of God which became his *stability* during dark and difficult days. It led to other personal, physical, and material benefits, but the spiritual benefits were the most valuable. Daniel learned how to persevere in prayer in his secret place, until he got the mind of God concerning the matters of life. So did Job, Abraham, David, Jeremiah, and Micah. It is a treasure of darkness that you can find too.

PERFECT PEACE

…that you may know that I, the Lord, who call you by your name, am the God of Israel. (Isa. 45:3)

God named Cyrus two centuries before Cyrus existed! He told Cyrus, through the scriptures, that "I have named you, though you have not known Me" (Isa. 45:4). Why? It was that God's Israel would be released from captivity and exile to return to their homeland to restore the temple (Isa. 44:28; 45:4) and so that Israel's God would be revealed as the only God (Isa. 45:3, 5) to the nations and people who did not yet know him. Cyrus did learn about this prophecy concerning him, and he fulfilled God's will according to what God purposed for him to do.

I believe that Cyrus came to know the God of Israel as Lord. In his first year as king of Persia, Cyrus issued a proclamation that said, "All the kingdoms of the earth the LORD God of heaven has given me. And He has commanded me to build Him a house at Jerusalem which is in Judah. Who is among you of all His people? May his God be with him, and let him go up to Jerusalem which is in Judah, and build the house of the LORD God of Israel (He is God), which is in Jerusalem" (Ezra 1:1-3; also given in 2 Chron. 36:22-23). This also fulfilled a prophecy made by the Lord through Jeremiah (Jer. 29:10). God had a special interest in and a very special purpose for Cyrus. Ultimately, God's desire was to reveal himself to Cyrus, and to all mankind, so that they would know that "there is no other God besides Me. Look to Me, a just God and Savior; there is none besides Me. Look to Me, and be saved, all you ends of the earth! For I am God, and there is no other" (Isa. 45:21-22).

Why did God want to reveal himself to mankind during the days of Cyrus, and why does he still desire to do so today? It is that they might be saved (2 Pet. 3:9). Cyrus was a type, or foreshadowing, of what God would ultimately and completely do through Christ. Isaiah went on to prophesy of the Messiah who would make it possible for mankind to receive eternal life in heaven. As sin separates man from God, so that he hides his face from us and cannot hear us (Isa. 59:2), Jesus died for our sins, for our deliverance, in order to bring us to God (Gal. 1:3; 1 Pet. 2:24; 3:18). Through believing in Jesus and what he did for us through his death and resurrection, we have peace with God. Our sins no longer put us at enmity with a just, holy God. Through his everlasting love for us (Jer. 31:3; John 3:16), God provided a way whereby we could have our *fellowship restored with him through Jesus.*

As all Christians have peace with God, not all Christians have the peace of God. Paul talked about the peace of God which surpasses all understanding (Phil. 4:7). It is a peace, though, that all Christians may not want to know. You see, there is a philosophy of Christianity today that preaches and teaches that sickness and suffering, distress and difficulties,

80

and trials and tribulation are not of God. It says that if you experience such things, it is because you lack faith. If this was a legitimate theological view, then most of Hebrews 11, the Hall of Faith chapter, would have to be removed from the Bible because most of those heroes of faith experienced great adversity.

To know the peace that passes all understanding requires trials that often bring suffering. The end result, though, is not a lack of faith, but there is the development of an unwavering, solid *faith that trusts completely in God* to see you through every circumstance and situation in life, no matter how trying and difficult they may be. You learn to be at peace, even in the midst of the storms of life. Instead of leaning to man's understanding, you learn to *follow God's understanding in all matters* (Prov. 3:5). That does not seem to be the norm for society today.

Isaiah referred to this level of peace in a similar, but different way, hundreds of years before Paul penned Philippians 4:7. Isaiah called it *perfect peace*. He said of God, "You will keep him in perfect peace, whose mind is stayed on You, because he trusts in You. Trust in the LORD forever, For in YAH, the LORD, is everlasting strength" (Isa. 26:3-4). Isaiah later wrote, "Who among you fears the LORD? Who obeys the voice of His Servant? Who walks in darkness and has no light? Let him trust in the name of the LORD and rely upon his God" (Isa. 50:10). It was mentioned in chapters two and four that the word translated "rely" in Isaiah 50:10 can also be translated, "stay." It is translated "lean" in Proverbs 3:5 and "stayed" in Isaiah 26:3. Isaiah and the writer in Proverbs have revealed to us that in divine darkness you are not to take matters into your own hands, but you are to place absolute trust and confidence in God, waiting for him to see you through. You are to stay upon God. The end result of that kind of trust in God is perfect peace.

God said, "I form the light and create darkness, I make peace and create calamity; I, the LORD do all these things" (Isa. 45:7). You can be sure that our God, who allows such diversity in life, wants us to be at peace. We find peace with God through Christ, and we reach perfect peace in God through Christ. It is a treasure of divine darkness because your eternal life through Christ is your strength and assurance in divine darkness that God is there, for the Bible says that God will not forsake those who are in Christ (John 10:27-30). The Lord has promised us that "I know the thoughts that I think toward you, . . . thoughts of peace and not of evil, to give you a future and a hope" (Jer. 29:11). God wants us to be at perfect peace. Divine darkness trains us to attain that level of maturity.

Yes, God does bring divine darkness upon you, but if you are exercised by it, you reach the level of peace that surpasses all understanding. To define this peace as simply as possible, I want to borrow from and expand a definition from the *The Liberty Bible Commentary* remarks on Philippians 4:7. This level of peace is "a state of spiritual and inward tranquility in which you are calm, contented, and at rest, even in the midst of trying circumstances, because your peace is grounded in God's presence, power, and promise."[5] A place where you find perfect peace is in divine darkness, where you cannot see God and feel his presence and power for a season of time. But you come to know that he is there, and that he is working according to the counsel and purpose of his will for your life (Eph. 1:11) and for your best (Rom. 8:28; Heb. 12:10). The process begins when your fellowship is restored with God through your professing Jesus as your Lord and Savior. You do not reach a level of faith that trusts completely in God and that follows God's understanding in all matters until your faith is tried and tested. Divine darkness is one way by which your faith is tried and tested. But it is necessary, if you want to find perfect peace. It is a wonderful state in which to be. Perfect peace is a "pearl of great price," a treasure of darkness, for those who have found it.

> *The treasures of darkness are really just basic fundamentals and truths of the Christian life that are available for us to use, but, so often, they are little used or unrealized in our lives.*

CONCLUSION

If you were expecting some new, great, profound truths to be revealed in this chapter, just remember these words of wisdom of Solomon: "There is nothing new under the sun" (Eccles. 1:9). The treasures of darkness are

---

5. Liberty Bible Commentary, Edward E. Hindson and Woodrow Michael Kroll, General Editors, Nelson Publishers, 1983, p. 2449.

really just basic fundamentals and truths of the Christian life that are available for us to use, but, so often, they are little used or unrealized in our lives. They become your treasures when you lay hold of them and live them out consistently in your life. We say that we believe in the perpetual presence of God and in his prevailing power. We talk about and even sing songs about the importance, necessity, and benefit of prayer, but how often do we really persevere in prayer? We know that we have peace with God, and we believe that we have peace in God, but how evident is perfect peace—the peace that surpasses all understanding—in your daily life and in the decisions you make? These "treasures" are too often neglected or ignored when everything is going our way and when we are basking in "heavenly sunlight" here on earth. And how wonderful his sunshine is! But our Father has to use his means of loving discipline to remind us to practice the spiritual basics that we need to make priorities in our lives.

The need of divine discipline is not a new concept. It is just a concept we have not taught much about in our day. It was known in the days of the Reformation, as exemplified through this quote that is credited to Martin Luther's wife: "I had never known . . . what such and such things meant, in such and such psalms, such complaints and workings of spirit; I had never understood the practices of Christian duties, had not God brought me under some affliction."[6]

Oswald Chambers has vividly described the benefit of the divine discipline of God, especially divine darkness:

> It is the glory of God to conceal His treasures in embarrassments, that is, in things that involve us in difficulty. "I will give you the treasures of darkness." We would never have suspected that treasures were hidden there, and in order to get them we have to go through things that involve us in perplexity. There is nothing more wearying to the eye than perpetual sunshine, and the same is true spiritually. The valley of the shadow gives us time to reflect, and we learn to praise God for the valley because in it our soul was restored in its communion with God. God gives us a new revelation of His kindness in the valley of the shadow. What are the days and the experiences that

---

6. Mrs. Charles Cowman, *Streams in the Desert: A Daily Devotional Journal* (Grand Rapids: Zondervan, 1965), 27.

have furthered us most? The days of green pastures, of absolute ease?
No, they have their value; but the days that have furthered us most
in character are the days of stress and cloud, the days when we could
not see our way but had to stand still and wait; and as we waited, the
comforting and sustaining and restoring of God came in a way we
never imagined possible before.[7]

I like the sunshine. I like the time of the year when the sun rises early in the morning and sets late in the evening. But I would not want sunshine twenty-four hours a day, for it is in the dark hours when I rest and gain strength to make it during the hours of light. I am glad that God made the day and the night.

It is the same spiritually. Those times of divine darkness are meant to provide spiritual rest, reflection, and revitalization, so that you go back into the light spiritually renewed, alert, and fit. The treasures of darkness are not those that will necessarily bring physical and material prosperity, but they are those that will bring the treasures which Jesus said are the richest: "Lay up for yourselves treasures in heaven, where neither moth nor rust destroys and where thieves do not break in and steal" (Matt. 6:20). Those are the treasures that matter the most. It is through those moments when you are isolated and insulated from the things of this world that you learn to treasure those things which are eternal. Divine darkness is such a place. You will never know its treasures until you have been there.

---

7. Oswald Chambers, *The Place of Help* (Grand Rapids: Discovery House, 1989), 90–91.

6: Divine Delay

"Getting in Stride with God"

Divine Delay: A period of time in which God keeps one waiting after he has heard God's original call regarding a matter.

Have you ever sensed God's guidance in a particular direction regarding a situation in your life, with an inner peace that the Lord is leading you in the decision you have made; yet, he keeps you waiting from seeing all the pieces fit together to bring about the fulfillment of what you believe God has revealed to you? Or maybe, you have been following God's will for your life, having steadfastly set your face to go in that direction, but an obstacle has been placed in your path that has slowed you down or even stopped your movement in that direction. Or, have you been praying about some areas of concern or about decisions facing you in life, yet you have not perceived any direction from the Lord, and you feel as if your prayers are not even being heard? If any of those scenarios applies to you, most likely you are experiencing the *divine discipline of delay.*

It has been said that there are four ways God answers our prayers: "yes," "no," "not now," and "you've got to be kidding!" Now we know that, as recorded in the Bible, the Lord never actually responded to a prayer request with that last answer, but in our human vernacular, "you've got to be kidding!" might have been an appropriate response to some requests. For instance, when Jesus was not received cordially by a Samaritan village, James and John wanted to pray down fire from heaven to destroy the village (see Luke 9:51-56). Jesus did not say, "you've got to be kidding!" but he did rebuke them for that suggestion, and he reminded them that he had not come to destroy men's lives but to save them.

Accordingly, we may not get the response to our prayers because of the nature of the request (1 John 5:14-15) and because of disobedience or unconfessed sin in our lives (Ps. 66:18). There are times, though, of divine delay regarding God's response to our prayers and the fulfillment of his will in our lives.

If you have not experienced divine delay, it will eventually occur in your life. If you allow it to exercise you and train you, divine delay will work for your benefit and for the benefit of others. We all tend to function around schedules that we do not want to have altered or delayed. Yet we would all have to admit that our schedules sometimes having been changed or interrupted have actually been to our advantage or for our safety. Some of the best and most meaningful moments of your life may have occurred because your schedule was altered. A schedule delay may even have saved your life. Whenever there has been a fatal jet crash, inevitably we will see someone interviewed who missed the departure of the ill-fated flight. Missing the departure of their flight was upsetting when it happened, but how thankful they were when they realized the thing that delayed them and caused them to miss their flight had kept them from death.

The divine discipline of delay is where great men and women of God are molded as you learn to completely lean on the Lord, trusting him to bring about what he has revealed to you or called you to do. A good example of divine delay is seen in the life of Moses. From his life we glean three purposes of divine delay: it deepens your communion with God; it develops your character for God; and it discloses your commitment to God.

GETTING IN STRIDE WITH GOD

In this chapter, we will examine divine delay in the life of Moses. The main three purposes of divine delay will be covered. In the first chapter of the book of Exodus, the Bible records that Pharaoh ordered the execution of the newborn sons of the Israelite slaves (Exod. 1:16). It was because the Egyptians feared the rapid multiplication of the Israelites could lead to their becoming mightier than these Egyptians who ruled the Israelites (Exod. 1:9-10). In a divine act of rescue (Exod. 2:1-10), a Hebrew baby boy, Moses, is discovered by the daughter of Pharaoh. She adopts him, and he grows us in Pharaoh's household. A day comes, after he grows up, when Moses goes back to his roots. Exodus 2:11-15 records the result of that encounter in the life of Moses:

> *Now it came to pass in those days, when Moses was grown, that he went out to his brethren and looked at their burdens. And he saw an Egyptian beating a Hebrew, one of his brethren. So he looked this way and that way, and when he saw no one, he killed the Egyptian and hid him in the sand. And when he went out the second day, behold, two Hebrew men were fighting, and he said to the one who did the wrong, "Why are you striking your companion?" Then he said, "Who made you a prince and a judge over us? Do you intend to kill me as you killed the Egyptian?" So Moses feared and said, "Surely this thing is known!" When Pharaoh heard of this matter, he sought to kill Moses. But Moses fled from the face of Pharaoh and dwelt in the land of Midian.*

Moses looked on the burdens of his people, and when he observed first hand one of its abuses, in the logic of the human flesh, he made an effort at being their deliverer. But he attacked physically, instead of spiritually! Even his fellow Hebrews, the ones for whom he had begun to fight, resented his initial efforts. God then sent Moses to the desert to be a shepherd for forty years: divine delay. At the end of that time, God appeared and told Moses to go and deliver his people out of slavery in Egypt (Exod. 3:1-10). Forty years earlier, the realization hit Moses that the direction his lot in life had taken—from a condemned baby, floating in a basket in a river, to the halls of Pharaoh's palace—may have been for him to be a deliverer for his people. But he was not yet ready. He needed to be divinely disciplined.

As a baby, God had already chosen Moses to be the one to lead the Israelites out of bondage. God divinely intervened to place Moses in a position where he could stand against the authority that had enslaved the Jews because he was at the highest levels of that authority. Moses was the right man for the job, but he still was not right for the job until he learned to *get in stride with God.* The Lord had to get the Egypt out of Moses so that Moses could get the Israelites out of Egypt. To lead his Hebrew brothers and sisters from slavery in Egypt would not happen by the force of human strength but by the power of spiritual might.

> ### The Lord had to get the Egypt out of Moses so that Moses could get the Israelites out of Egypt.

There were three areas of Moses' life where he needed to be exercised and trained during his forty years of divine delay. They give three reasons for which God may bring divine delay into your life: to deepen your communion with God; to develop your character for God; and to disclose your commitment to God.

DEEPENS YOUR COMMUNION WITH GOD

To get in stride with God, Moses first had to get to know about God, and then he had to get to know God. Communion, in its spiritual sense, is open, honest, intimate fellowship with the Lord. As divine delay may come into your life for you to *deepen your communion with God*, it is a time to review, a time to remove, and a time to renew.

A shepherd spent many hours, even days and weeks, away from the mainstream activities of life, as he led his sheep to feed in fertile pastures. A shepherd had plenty of time just to think. In those quiet, secluded feeding grounds, Moses had time to commune with God, after he got to know God. But even before he really got to know God, Moses surely used those hours and days as *a time to review* his life. He must have thought often of those years when, as the adopted son of Pharaoh's daughter, he had the finest of everything and anything he wanted as a member of the most powerful family in Egypt. Now here he was, leading around a flock of smelly sheep, with the ground for his bed and the sun by day and the stars by night as a roof.

We can surmise that, through this process, Moses learned not to think too much of himself and what he could accomplish in the strength of his flesh. Moses had forty years to review his life so that when the call came from God, he answered, "Who am I that I should go to Pharaoh, and that I should bring the children of Israel out of Egypt?" (Exod. 3:11). When we realize how unqualified we are apart from God, and how dependent we are upon God, that is when he can best use us. Divine delay is a time to review where you have been in your life, what you are presently doing, and who it has made you. It is to get you to the place of realizing that you are nothing apart from the presence of God in your life and from following his direction for your life.

As you review your life during divine delay, it is *a time to remove* those things from your life that hold a greater place of importance than your relationship with the Lord and the fulfillment of his will for your life. Beyond the time of the text in Exodus, God would later tell the freed Israelites to "love the LORD your God with all your heart, with all your soul, and with all your strength" (Deut. 6:5). Jesus reconfirmed the priority of that command when he said that it was the greatest commandment of all (Matt. 22:36-38). What needs to be removed from your life so that you love the Lord with all your heart, soul, and mind?

You need to remove what halts your walk with God. Undealt with sin will do that in the life of a Christian—it halts your walk with the Lord. Your prayers are hindered (Ps. 66:18), and you do not sense the joy of the Lord and the filling of the Holy Spirit. But as you confess and repent of sin in your life (1 John 1:9), God forgives you and cleanses you from the unrighteousness of your sins. You can be assured that your walk with God will be restored. God gives us his Word:

> *If you walk in My statutes and keep My commandments, and perform them, . . . I will walk among you and be your God, and you shall be My people.* (Lev. 26:3, 12)

> *For the LORD your God walks in the midst of your camp, to deliver you and give your enemies over to you; therefore your camp shall be holy, that He may see no unclean thing among you, and turn away from you.* (Deut. 23:14)

God says that he will walk with you, but it is dependent upon your obedience to his Word. When you allow things to become a part of your life which are contrary to the Word of God, it affects your walk with him.

To deepen your communion with God, you also need to remove what hinders your work for God. The apostle Paul said, "But one thing I do" (Phil. 3:13). There are many things you can get involved with in your work for the Lord. But it may be to the extent that you are not effectively doing the work of the Lord. It is best to center your abilities where you can be most effective for God. You may need to remove some areas of involvement from your schedule in order to give of your best in those areas where you are most gifted. If you feel led to give up involvement in something God wants done, then he will find someone to replace you in that particular area of service. Especially be careful in your involvement in secular activities. You may find yourself so involved with school activities, sports teams, civic organizations, social groups, and your job that your work for the Lord has to give way over and over again to your secular involvement. You may be in divine delay right now so that you will review and remove those things from your life, some that are not necessarily bad, but they are things which hinder your work for God.

If you are in divine delay, it may have come upon your life to get you to remove those things that negatively affect your communion with the Lord and your witness for him.

You also need to remove from your life what hurts your witness for God. You can have a walk with the Lord and an effective work for God, yet there can be something in your life that is hurting your witness for God. Our communion with God is harmed when we allow things to be a part of our life that ought not to be. If you are in divine delay, it may have come upon your life to get you to remove those things that negatively affect your communion with the Lord and your witness for him.

Divine delay is also *a time to renew* yourself in the Lord. As you review your life and remove spiritually detrimental things from your life, there is a renewal in your relationship with the Lord. It results in a deepening of your communion with God.

What exactly needs to be renewed in your life? There are at least three areas where renewal, in those areas, will have a positive effect over every other area of your life. Divine delay is a time to "be transformed by the renewing of your *mind*, that you may prove what is that good and acceptable and perfect will of God" (Rom. 12:2). It is a time to renew your *mouth* for God so that the words of your mouth and the meditation of your heart will be acceptable and pleasing to the Lord (Ps. 19:14). Divine delay is also a time to renew your *mission* for God so that God is working "in you both to will and to do for His good pleasure" (Phil. 2:13). Oswald Chambers gave this summary of the exile years of Moses:

> *We may have the vision of God and a very clear understanding of what God wants, and we start to do the thing, then comes something equivalent to the forty years in the wilderness, as if God had ignored the whole thing, and when we are thoroughly discouraged God comes back and revives the call, and we get the quaver in and say—"Oh, who am I?" We have to learn the first great stride of God—"I AM WHO I AM has sent me." We have to learn that our individual effort for God is an impertinence; our individuality is to be rendered incandescent by a personal relationship to God (see Matthew 3:17). We fix on the individual aspect of things; we have the vision—"This is what God wants me to do;" but we have not got into God's stride.*[8]

Moses had forty years to review his life, and that is how long it took to remove from Moses what needed to be removed to get him in stride with God. Moses came out of the desert a renewed man. He went into the desert strong in the flesh, but he came out of the desert mighty in the Spirit of God. He had died to his old nature of position, prominence, and pride. He probably sensed forty years earlier that he was the right man to lead his people out of bondage, but now he was right for leading them to do it. The Bibles says of Moses that he was the most humble man on the earth (Num. 12:3) and that there was not another prophet like him whom the Lord knew face to face (Deut. 34:10). During the time of divine delay in his life, Moses learned communion with God, and he lived it the rest of his life.

---

8.   Chambers, *My Utmost for His Highest*, 212.

DEVELOPS YOUR CHARACTER FOR GOD

If you are going through a time of divine delay, there is a big, personal enlargement ahead for you. That personal enlargement may be of great benefit to others. The spiritual enlargement that Moses gained during divine delay benefitted an entire nation. But you must avoid getting dejected and discouraged during a time of divine delay. Let it be a time of striving to get in stride with God by daily meeting with him in his Word and in prayer (communion with God). As divine delay may come to discipline you in your prayer life and in your service to the Lord, it also *develops your character for God*. Divine delay develops your character for God to be what God wants you to be, to be where God wants you to be, and to be who God wants you to be.

Success, God's way, is based on what you are. In the eyes of the world, the standard for success, unfortunately, is based on where you are and who you are. A title someone has gained, a position that has been attained, even an inherited name, may bring recognition, notoriety, and prestige in man's eyes; yet in God's eyes, it does not mean much at all. Some of today's prominent and well-known individuals have become who they are and gotten where they are by walking all over others, by being unethical and immoral, and by disobeying other biblical principles and standards. Such individuals cannot influence this world to a saving knowledge of Jesus Christ with that kind of character. If God has allowed us a place of prominence in life, it is that we might use that position as a means of witness for Jesus. Divine delay may occur in your life so that God can develop your character *to be what He wants you to be*.

> *God is more concerned with what you are than where you are and who you are.*

God is more concerned with what you are than where you are and who you are. Being the adopted son of Pharaoh's daughter and growing up in the royal family did not qualify Moses to be the one to lead his people out of bondage. It worked to his advantage, for although he was a Hebrew, he was not a slave like his fellow Jews. Thus, he had freedom to go where he needed to go to negotiate on behalf of the Israelites. But he first had to become what God wanted him to be spiritually in order to act on behalf of God, in the Lord's will, to free the Israelites from bondage.

Although God is the most concerned with what you are, he does desire for you *to be where he wants you to be*. There is a specific place where God wants you to fulfill his will for your life, but again, his chief concern is that you will get to the point in your life that you will do the *what* of the will of God, regardless of where you may presently be.

Are you willing to go where God wants you to go without regard to salary, without regard to safety, and without regard to season? Such willingness is exemplified in the life of Paul. When Paul did not receive enough financial support to meet his needs from those he ministered to, he worked as a tentmaker to support himself financially so that he could preach the gospel (see Acts 18:3-4). But even when that was not possible, he was determined to go where God wanted him to go without regard to salary. The dedication of Paul to that commitment was evident in his letter to the church at Philippi, as he wrote, "For I have learned in whatever state I am, to be content: I know how to be abased, and I know how to abound. Everywhere and in all things I have learned both to be full and to be hungry, both to abound and to suffer need" (Phil. 4:11-12).

Paul went where God wanted him to go without regard to safety (see Acts 14:19-20; 16:22-24; 20:18-19; 21:13; 2 Tim. 3:10-12). He was willing to go wherever God wanted him to go, even if it cost him his life! Paul encouraged his son in the ministry, Timothy, on how to live out his life without regard to safety. He informed Timothy that "all who desire to live godly in Christ Jesus will suffer persecution" (2 Tim. 3:12). Paul knew, as long as he was going where God wanted him to go, he could also encourage Timothy to do the same, as Paul acknowledged, "Persecutions, afflictions, which happened to me at Antioch, at Iconium, at Lystra—what persecutions I endured. And out of them all the Lord delivered me" (2 Tim. 3:11).

Paul went where God wanted him to go without regard to season. He exhorted Timothy to "Preach the word! Be ready in season and out of season" (2 Tim. 4:2). Paul learned to make it the right season to preach Jesus whether conditions were spiritually ripe or not.

You may be wondering why Paul has been used as an example for a concept learned from the life of Moses. It is because Paul has provided many scripture verses that exhort us to live these principles which were first lived out hundreds of years before in the life of Moses. As Moses allowed divine delay to exercise him for its intended purpose, his character was so developed for God that he was willing to go where God wanted him to go without regard to safety, salary, or season. He was willing to go back where, at one time, they wanted to kill him (Exod. 2:15). God had told Moses that all the men who had sought to kill him were dead. But still, it was probably in the back of Moses' mind that there were family members of those who had sought to kill him who knew of him. The story of Moses would have been passed down from the generational peers of Moses to their children and grandchildren. There would also be legal and historical records concerning the murder and escape Moses had committed forty years before. Divine delay had trained Moses, though, to go where God wanted him to go without regard to safety.

Moses was willing to go where God wanted him to go without regard to salary. Other than God's promise to him that "I will certainly be with you" (Exod. 3:12), Moses had no assurance of income when he accepted the job to lead the Israelites out of bondage. All he had was a shepherd's rod. But it would become virtually priceless because of the powers God worked through it (see Exod. 4:2-4; 14:16; 17:5-6; Num. 20:8-11). Moses learned, from the day he became what God wanted him to be, and from the day he committed to go where God wanted him to go, that God's presence would provide for everything he needed (Deut. 2:7). Through his obedience to follow the will of God for his life, an entire nation learned that God would provide for all their needs, even if he needed to "rain bread from heaven" (Exod. 16:4). His provision was sent for one day at a time, seasonally, or provided before it was needed (Deut. 28:1-13). It was conditional, though, upon their obedience to God (Deut. 28:13-14).

Moses was willing to go where God wanted him to go without regard to season. The Lord told him, at the outset, "The king of Egypt will not let you go, no, not even by a mighty hand" (Exod. 3:19). It was going to take some time, and there would be difficulties to endure, waiting for the season to come when Pharaoh would say, "Rise, go out among my people, both you and the children of Israel" (Exod. 12:31).

God is also concerned with who you are. The name you bear brings a positive or negative mental reaction every time someone hears your name or sees it in print. The Bible says, "A good name is rather to be chosen than great riches, loving favor rather than silver and gold" (Prov. 22:1). A "good name" has been defined as "a title that inspires confidence, because the person behind it can be consistently depended upon to do what is legally and morally right, whatever the cost."[9] The reaction your name brings can be affected by your actions and the past actions of other family members who have the same last name. You can build a good name where you may have a bad name because of actions by you or other members of your family. In one generation, a good name can be destroyed, a bad name can be redeemed, or a good name can continue on for another generation. It depends on your allowing God to develop your character *to be who God wants you to be.*

You need to be who God wants you to be in your attitude, your ambitions, and your actions. The name you inherit will be identified with the character of your parents, grandparents, and other family members. But your name will ultimately be identified by your character. A good name is dependent on your attitude. The Bible says of a person, "For as he thinks in his heart, so is he" (Prov. 23:7). What you are on the inside will ultimately show through on the outside. Your attitude influences your ambition. If your attitude is in accord with what honors God, then your ambition in life will be to fulfill God's will for your life. You will not have to get what you want, when you want it, and where you want it at the expense of others. Even though there may times that you will stumble, your good name will endure (Prov. 24:16). Attitude and ambition will influence your actions. If you are who God wants you to be in your attitude and ambition, then your actions will testify as to whose you are and your life will be a witness for Christ (1 Cor. 10:31–11:1; Col. 3:17).

The name of Moses took on a new meaning when he returned to Egypt. Forty years earlier, the name of Moses meant "murderer" to the Egyptians, and it brought resentful thoughts to the Hebrews. But when he returned, the name Moses would come to mean "spokesman for God" to the Egyptians, and "deliverer" on behalf of God to the Israelites. Moses returned to Egypt, not as a member of the royal family, but as a servant of God, speaking for God on behalf of his oppressed people. Who Moses was then took on greater significance because of what he was. Divine delay had developed Moses' character for God.

---

9. *Men's Manual*, Vol. II; Institute In Basic Youth Conflicts (Oak Brook, Illinois, 1983) 183.

DISCLOSES YOUR COMMITMENT TO GOD

Divine delay not only deepens your communion with God and develops your character for God, but it also *discloses your commitment to God.* Divine delay allows you to see yourself as you really are in your commitment to God. During divine delay, you will either falter, fall apart, flee, or continue to follow God. Moses could very easily have faltered, fallen apart, or fled during the process of God's call upon his life to get the Israelites freed from bondage and to lead them to the Promised Land. But he followed God, so that the Lord was able to say of him, "He is faithful" (Num. 12:7). Divine delay discloses your commitment to God in the whatever, wherever, and whenever of his will for your life.

Divine delay discloses your commitment to God in *the whatever of his will for your life.* God wants to work in you both to will and to do for his good pleasure (Phil. 2:13). Are you committed to him in whatever situation you may find yourself? If you are praying according to the will of God, and you do not have unconfessed and undealt with sins in your life, yet you find yourself in divine delay, then just continue to follow God. Delight yourself in him and in your

> *Divine delay allows you to see yourself as you really are in your commitment to God.*

service for him, and the Bible says that he will give you the desires of your heart (Ps. 37:4). But he will do so in his time. If you are doing the whatever of God's will for your life, then his desires will be your desires. You can be assured that God will bring about what he has purposed to do (Eph. 1:9-11).

Moses questioned the choice of God in choosing him for the special assignment of leading the children of Israel from oppression in Egypt. But God had told him, "Come now, therefore, and I will send you to Pharaoh that you may bring My people, the children of Israel, out of Egypt" (Exod. 3:10). Because divine delay had deepened his communion with God and had developed his character for God, Moses reluctantly accepted the special call of God. As we learn from the rest of the story, God was powerfully present with Moses to help him fulfill a great mission. But the initial reluctance of Moses did displease God. Let us resolve to readily accept God's call to us, whatever it may be.

Divine delay also discloses your commitment to God in *the wherever of his will for your life*. Are you truly willing to follow him wherever he leads you? God told Moses to go and return to Egypt to bring the Israelites out of bondage. Moses was hesitant, at first, because he was unsure of his abilities at that point of his life. But that was where God wanted him. God did not want Moses' abilities as much as he wanted his availability. If God says to "go," you can be assured that he will equip you with everything you need to fulfill his will (Heb. 13:21).

God told Moses to go back to the place from which he had run away. Forty years earlier, he had left there as a felon and as a failure in the eyes of many people. But God sent him back. And the Bible records that he did: "And the LORD said to Moses in Midian, 'Go, return to Egypt; for all the men who sought your life are dead.' Then Moses took his wife and his sons and set them on a donkey, and he returned to the land of Egypt" (Exod. 4:19-20).

Divine delay also discloses your commitment to God in *the whenever of his will for your life*. Are you committed to go when God calls you to go? Complete obedience to God is doing exactly what he says to do, when he says to do it, without questioning what he has asked you to do. It is to have the right heart attitude in accepting and carrying out God's will for your life. Moses did question God, and even made excuses about his lack of abilities, especially as a speaker (Exod. 4:10). But where God guides, God provides. God provided someone to help Moses—his brother, Aaron—so that he could effectively communicate. The Lord told Moses, "Is not Aaron the Levite your brother? I know that he can speak well. And look, he is also coming out to meet you. When he sees you, he will be glad in his heart. Now you shall speak to him and put the words in his mouth. And I will be with your mouth and with his mouth, and I will teach you what you shall do. So he shall be your spokesman to the people. And he himself shall be as a mouth for you, and you shall be to him as God" (Exod. 4:14-16).

The Lord will do the same for you, if he has called you to do something and you do not feel that you can do it. He will give you the ability and the resources to do it, or he will provide you with helpers who will assist you and follow your leadership.

CONCLUSION

Divine delay, like all the divine disciplines, will greatly test your patience. You must avoid getting dejected, depressed, and discouraged during a time of divine delay. In the words of Oswald Chambers,

> *Anything that savors of dejection spiritually is always wrong. If depression and oppression visit me, I am to blame; God is not, nor is anyone else. Dejection springs from one of two sources—I have either satisfied a lust or I have not. Lust means—I must have it at once. Spiritual lust demands an answer from God, instead of seeking God Who gives the answer. . . . Whenever the insistence is on the point that God answers prayer, we are off track. The meaning of prayer is that we get hold of God, not the answer.*[10]

Do not be guilty of spiritual lust during divine delay. Remember, God is working for your benefit and the benefit of others during divine delay. Use it as a time in your life to "get hold of God."

If you allow divine delay to exercise you as it is intended to do, it will deepen your communion with God so that you get in stride with him and stay in his great stride. A big, personal, spiritual enlargement is ahead of you that will be of great benefit to others. But your character must first be developed according to God's design. Through the whole process, you will learn how committed you are as a Christian.

> *Get in stride with God, and the whatever, wherever, and whenever of the will of God will come together in the right way, the right place, and the right time.*

Too many Christians are committed in serving the Lord, as long as everything goes well or according to the way "I want it to go." When a Christian's commitment is that shallow, he is of little use for the cause of Christ. Maybe you are still in divine delay because your dejection, depression, disobedience, impatience, and insensitivity are in opposition to how God is wanting to mold you. Get in stride with God, and the whatever, wherever, and whenever of the will of God will come together in the right way, the right place, and the right time.

---

10. Chambers, *My Utmost for His Highest*, 27.

7: Divine Differences

"What Is That to You?"

Divine Differences: *The process of how God's calling for one's life does not appear to be fair in comparison to how others in a similar position appear to be treated by God.*

Perhaps you have heard the statement, "God treats everyone equally." Regarding what is most important in life, eternal salvation, there is equality in how one receives the forgiveness of sins and the free gift of eternal life in heaven (Rom. 10:9-13). It is true that "the ground is level at the foot of the cross." But there are areas of life where there is not level ground, at least by human standards, which God knows about and even allows. For example, there are rich and poor (Prov. 22:2), and Jesus acknowledged it would always be that way (Matt. 26:11; Mark 14:7; John 12:8).

The calling of God differs in our lives. He does not call every person to make it to the top in one's profession. God calls some to the middle, and most of us will find ourselves on the lower rungs of the corporate ladder or in our particular occupation. The reason, though, that some individuals make it better than others is not always because of their calling or station in life. For example, some athletes excel more than others of equal or greater abilities because they work at it harder and longer in practice and training. Effort often has more to do with success than calling or ability.

There is a divine difference, though, where two individuals are well-qualified for a task, and both desire to do it, but God only chooses one for the task. When it was time for a successor to Moses as the leader of Israel, God chose Joshua, although Caleb also appeared to be well qualified for the job. He certainly had proven that he was as faithful and brave as Joshua (Num. 13:30; 14:6-9, 24). The Lord's choice of Joshua over Caleb is an example of *divine differences in position*. God may also allow an individual or group to experience great suffering and persecution, while their peers in a similar position suffer little, if at all. In the twelfth chapter of Acts, when Herod sought to put James and Peter to death, God allowed James to be killed, but he rescued Peter. That incident gives an illustration of *divine differences in persecution*. There is also *divine differences in personality*, which is seen in the way God worked through personalities such as John and Peter.

All three aspects of divine differences are found in an incident involving Jesus, Peter, and John, as recorded in John 21:18-23.

> *"Most assuredly, I say to you, when you were younger, you girded yourself and walked where you wished; but when you are old, you will stretch out your hands, and another will gird you and carry you where you do not wish." This He spoke, signifying by what death he would glorify God. And when He had spoken this, He said to him, "Follow Me."*

> *Then Peter, turning around, saw the disciple whom Jesus loved following, who also had leaned on His breast at the supper, and said, "Lord, who is the one who betrays You?" Peter, seeing him, said to Jesus, "But Lord, what about this man?"*

> *Jesus said to him, "If I will that he remain till I come, what is that to you? You follow Me." Then this saying went out among the brethren that this disciple would not die. Yet Jesus did not say to him that he would not die, but, "If I will that he remain till I come, what is that to you?"*

This conversation between Jesus and Peter occurred after the resurrection of the Lord during one of the special appearances Christ made to his followers prior to his ascension. This particular incident was the Lord's way of dealing with the stigma of Peter's denial of him by lovingly restoring fellowship with Peter and readying him for future service. In verses eighteen and nineteen, Jesus indicated how Peter's life would end. Tradition reveals that Peter died for his faith in Christ by being crucified upside down. When he was sentenced to death by crucifixion, he asked to be crucified upside down because he did not feel worthy to die as Jesus had. But Peter wanted to know how John would die, so he posed that question to the Lord. Jesus replied, "What is that to you?" The Lord told Peter that how he chose to deal with John should not be of concern to Peter. Jesus said what Peter needed to be concerned with above all else was this, "You follow Me" (John 21:22).

Divine Differences

In this account, the Bible gives an example of divine differences. God's will for our lives differs, and it is seen in the different ways God uses us from others who may even share the same calling or vocation in life. Peter later emerged as the main spokesman for the early church, and he was in that intimate circle with James and John, who had a closer relationship with Jesus than the other disciples during the earthly life of Christ. John, though, apparently had a special relationship with the Lord more so than Peter or the other disciples. The Bible refers to John as the "disciple whom Jesus loved" (John 13:23; 19:26; 20:2; 21:20). While he was on the cross, Jesus told his mother to love John like a son, and he told John to take Mary into his home as if she was his mother (John 19:25-27). It appeared that John had the closest friendship with Jesus of all the disciples. This illustrates divine differences in position.

Peter and John also provide an example of divine differences in persecution. Peter was martyred for being a follower of Christ. Tradition holds that although John was exiled to Patmos for being a follower of Jesus, he did return to Ephesus, where he died a normal death in old age near the end of the first century.

Divine differences in personality is also applicable in comparing the lives of

> *God's will for our lives differs, and it is seen in the different ways God uses us from others who may even share the same calling or vocation in life.*

101

Peter and John. During the earthly days of our Lord, Peter was often the recipient of stern comments from Jesus. Peter's personality was such that he was usually the first one to comment on a matter, or he was the first one to answer when the Lord asked a question. There were times when he did not think matters through, and his sincere but sincerely wrong replies received reprimands from Jesus. Even in the passage from John 21, the Lord rebuked Peter for being sidetracked with John's future (John 21:22) when Jesus was dealing with Peter's life. Because of Peter's strong and impulsive personality, it seems that more comments are made in sermons and books about Peter's shortcomings than any other disciple with the exception of Judas Iscariot. Although there was a time when the Lord rebuked John (Luke 9:55) and his brother, James, we do not hear comments about any negative traits John may have had because his personality did not lean to it as did Peter's.

As our individual callings in life differ, you may find yourself on what you feel to be the harder end of divine differences. If that is the case, it is not something to feel rejected about, but it could be a reason to rejoice. We will learn why as we examine the divine discipline of differences.

DIVINE DIFFERENCES IN POSITION

As mentioned in the chapter introduction, a biblical example of divine differences in position is seen in the lives of Caleb and Joshua. Of the twelve spies sent out to scout the land of Canaan, Caleb and Joshua were the only ones who believed the Israelites could go in as God had promised and militarily claim the Promised Land. As punishment for their lack of trust in God, the rest of the Israelites over twenty years of age died during forty years of wandering in the desert, not permitted to enter the Promised Land. Caleb and Joshua were allowed to settle their families into Canaan because they had been faithful and obedient to God. When it was time for a new leader of Israel, God chose Joshua to succeed Moses, although Caleb appeared to be just as qualified for the position. Now the Bible does not give any indication that Caleb aspired to succeed Moses, but if that had been his desire, it is evident that he did not allow it to make him bitter, resentful, and uncooperative.

He remained loyal to his people and to God. Some beneficial character lessons and qualities can be learned from the life of Caleb that can help you if you have been passed over for a position that you greatly desired.

One lesson we can learn from Caleb is that *humility is more important than the prestige you have gained*. The Bible says that "God resists the proud but gives grace to the humble" (Prov. 3:34; James 4:6; 1 Pet. 5:5). Caleb's actions, reactions, and responses to circumstances in his life showed that he was a humble man, although he was a man who had gained prestige.

By the time the Israelites had wandered forty years and were about to enter the Promised Land, Joshua and Caleb would have been folk heroes. The people knew that these two men and their respective families were going to be allowed what even Moses was not allowed to do: enter and live in the Promised Land. The people knew that Joshua and Caleb had remained true and obedient to God when their fellow spies had led the rest of the people to rebel against God's will.

Joshua had now become the leader of Israel and the more prominent of the two, but Caleb's total commitment to God was known throughout the nation of Israel. Six times the Bible states that Caleb "wholly followed the Lord." When the spies returned from their mission into Canaan, Caleb was the spy who "quieted the people before Moses, and said, 'Let us go up at once and take possession, for we are well able to overcome it'" (Num.13:30). Joshua stood with Caleb when the people followed the advice of the other ten spies who said, "We are not able to go up against the people, for they are stronger than we" (Num.13:31). In this particular incident, Caleb must have been the more prominent figure because he was the principal spokesman, and God did single him out for his courage and commitment (Num.14:24). But as the Israelites prepared to enter Canaan, Joshua had emerged into the more prestigious position.

Your station and position in life may change at any moment. You can go from the top to the bottom as quickly as from the bottom to the top. You can go from being an "unknown" in your career to an "overnight success" through a stroke of fate. But there is always someone waiting in the wings to knock you from the number one position. Caleb simply accepted the higher position of leadership God gave to Joshua. He did not fret and pout over the reality that someone else got a position that he may have been capable of fulfilling. He did not get bitter, envious, or resentful.

Caleb continued fulfilling the lot in life to which God had called him. When the land divisions in Canaan were being assigned to the Israelites, Caleb respectfully came before Joshua to ask for the land he had been promised forty-five years earlier (Josh. 14:6-15). At eighty-five years of age, he was "wholly following the Lord" as he was when he was forty. Caleb had a reverent respect for God and God's divine differences in position.

As Caleb accepted his position in life, and as he respected the position of others, he was recognized for it. Joshua 14:13 says that Joshua blessed Caleb and gave him the land he had requested. God had promised the land to Caleb (Deut. 1:36), Moses confirmed it, and Joshua officially sanctioned it. Caleb was recognized and honored by the highest officials of his nation. The Bible says that "before honor is humility" (Prov. 15:33; 18:12). The Bible also promises, "By humility and the fear of the Lord are riches and honor and life" (Prov. 22:4). Caleb was a famous man, but he was a humble man. It brought him honor from the Lord and from his fellow man. It also kept him healthy, for at eighty-five he was just as fit as at forty (Josh. 14:11), and he received his riches through the land and the home that he provided for his family in the Promised Land.

> *If you please God, it does not matter whom you displease; but if you displease God, it does not matter whom you please.*

A second beneficial character lesson learned from the life of Caleb is that *identity is more important than the position you have attained.* Caleb had attained a position of leadership in his tribe of Israel. Only one man was selected from each tribe to spy out the land of Canaan, "everyone a leader among them" (Num.13:1). But the position of leadership he had attained did not really matter when the people of Israel disagreed with the report he gave. The people wanted to kill Caleb and Joshua (Num. 14:10), but the Lord intervened on behalf of those who trusted in him. To Caleb, it was more important to be identified as one who wholly followed the Lord than one who was popular with the crowd because he did what pleased them.

I have heard it said that if you please God, it does not matter whom you displease; but if you displease God, it does not matter whom you please. How does God know you? We know how God knew Caleb. He knew him as one who "has a different spirit in him and he has followed me fully" (Num. 14:24). How do others know you? Moses knew Caleb as one who "wholly followed the Lord" (Num. 32:12). Joshua knew Caleb as one who "wholly followed the Lord" (Josh. 14:14). As it was brought to their attention on at least three occasions, the children of Israel knew that Caleb "wholly followed the Lord." What a wonderful way to be identified by others and by God. But it is not only important how others identify you, but how you identify yourself. Caleb said of himself, "I have wholly followed the Lord my God" (Josh. 14:9). What a marvelous testimony! At age forty, Caleb had wholly followed the Lord, and when he was over twice that age, Caleb had a testimony that was still making a difference for the Lord in his life and in the lives of others. That was more important to him than any position of fame and fortune he may have attained.

A third lesson that we can learn from Caleb to help us in dealing with divine differences in position is that *integrity is more important than the principle you have claimed.* Caleb was a man of integrity. When a Bible personality has as many references about them as Caleb, usually there is at least one recorded instance where that person made a mistake. But that is not the case with Caleb. Oh, he made mistakes in his life, but that is not what he was remembered for. He was steady and consistent in his walk with the Lord.

Caleb waited forty-five years to get what was rightfully his. While he was waiting to receive his inheritance, he continued to fulfill his responsibilities. When the time came, and it was right to do so, he went through the proper channels in the proper way to claim what was rightfully his. Credibility mattered to him, for he was a man of integrity, and it was evident in his character and in his conduct. Caleb was identified by God, by others, and even by himself for what he was—a man who wholly followed the Lord. Caleb never asked God to make him the leader of Israel, and he did not indicate that as being a desire of his life. He appeared to be qualified for the position, but he was not God's man for the position. So Caleb simply accepted the position to which God had called him in life.

Caleb did claim his inheritance in the Promised Land, with the help of a young man named Othniel, who became his son-in-law. Caleb even outlived Joshua. After Joshua's death, the Israelites continued to serve the Lord, as long as the elders who outlived Joshua were alive (Judg. 2:7). The Bible does not single out a leader of Israel during that time. But after the elders died, the Bible says that the children of Israel did evil in the sight of the Lord (Judg. 3:7). So the Lord allowed them to be under the control of the king of Mesopotamia. But the Lord eventually raised a deliverer for them. It was Othniel, the son-in-law of Caleb. He was the leader of Israel for forty years. Caleb never was the highest ranking official in Israel, but one of the rewards of his having been wholly committed to God was that his daughter became the "first lady" of Israel. During the forty years of her husband's leadership over Israel, the land had rest for forty years (Judg. 3:11). Caleb's heirs were able to enjoy in peace the inheritance he had provided for them.

DIVINE DIFFERENCES IN PERSECUTION

From the text in John 21, which was used to introduce us to the divine discipline of differences, Jesus told Peter how he would die. The Bible says, "'Most assuredly, I say to you, when you were younger, you girded yourself and walked where you wished; but when you are old, you will stretch out your hands, and another will gird you and carry you where you do not wish.' This He spoke, signifying by what death he would glorify God" (John 21:18-19). Jesus said that Peter's death would come about as a result of persecution, and like the Lord, Peter would be crucified. When Peter inquired as to how John would die, the Lord replied, "What is that to you? You follow Me" (John 21:22). Jesus was getting Peter to realize that what mattered the most was for him to fulfill the Lord's will for his life regardless of how the Lord dealt with someone else's life. Peter was martyred for being a follower of Christ. John was exiled to the Island of Patmos for being a follower of Jesus, but he was allowed to return to Ephesus, in his in his old age, where he died a normal death near the end of the first century.

This incident introduces us to a second kind of divine difference that you may experience: *divine differences in persecution*. Peter appeared to receive the unfair side of divine differences in persecution in comparing his life with John's. But on another occasion, God spared the life of Peter while allowing James, John's brother, to be killed. In the twelfth chapter of Acts, it is recorded that King Herod began to arrest believers in Christ, and he had James, the brother of John, put to death (Acts 12:1-2). Herod had Peter arrested too, intending to execute him. But fervent prayer was made on behalf of Peter (Acts 12:5). The night before he was to be executed, an angel of the Lord came to Peter in his cell where he was chained to two soldiers. Peter's chains fell off, and the angel led him safely out of the prison. He then went to Mary's home, the mother of John Mark, where the inner circle of believers were gathered for prayer. At first they did not believe the very thing they were praying for had occurred. They thought it was his ghost. But Peter assured them that he had been rescued by the Lord. He departed and went to another place (see Acts 12:1-17 for the full account of this story). Throughout the rest of his life, he continued to proclaim the good news of Jesus.

Another relevant incident concerning divine differences in persecution is given in the sixth and seventh chapters of Acts. In these chapters, the Bible gives an account of Stephen, one of the first seven deacons of the early church. Stephen quickly achieved prominence for aggressive, vigorous evangelism and powerful preaching. The Bible described him as one who was full of faith and power, who was able to perform great wonders and miracles ("signs") among the people (Acts 6:8). Some unbelieving Jews could not argue with him because he spoke in the wisdom and power of the Holy Spirit. So they rose up against Stephen. They had false witnesses rise up too against Stephen, and he was brought before the Council (Sanhedrin) that had condemned Christ. Chapter seven of Acts records a mighty sermon he preached before the Sanhedrin, which so convicted them that they could not stand it. So they took Stephen out of the city and stoned him to death. The Bible says that throughout this ordeal, Stephen was full of the Holy Spirit (Acts 7:55). He even asked the Lord, just before he died, not to charge his executioners with this sin (Acts 7:60).

As we read through the book of Acts, we see that James was killed, Stephen was killed, Peter was spared, and as we get to the life of Paul, his life was spared. He is still alive at the end of Acts, although he suffered greatly, at times, for the cause of Christ. Were James and Stephen less right with God? Were Peter and Paul more favored with God? As their lives were spared through the years covered in the account of Acts, eventually Peter and Paul were both martyred for the Lord. But none of those men just mentioned had more favor with God than the others. As there are divine differences of position in life, there are also divine differences regarding persecution. Why does God allow some to suffer in life for the cause of Christ, and what good could it bring about?

Three purposes for divine differences in persecution are found in the book of Acts. The first instance recorded in Acts, where believers were persecuted by a legal system for believing in Jesus, is in the fourth chapter. The Bible says about Peter and John,

> *Now as they spoke to the people, the priests, the captain of the temple, and the Sadducees came upon them, being greatly disturbed that they taught the people and preached in Jesus the resurrection from the dead. And they laid hands on them, and put them in custody until the next day, for it was already evening. (Acts 4:1-3)*

Peter and John were detained by the authorities overnight. When they were brought before the authorities the next day, they were asked, "By what power or by what name have you done this?" Peter replied, "Let it be known to you all, and to all the people of Israel, that

> *Why does God allow some to suffer in life for the cause of Christ?*

by the name of Jesus Christ of Nazareth, whom you crucified, whom God raised from the dead, by Him this man stands here before you whole" (Acts 4:10). Peter revealed where their power came from. He acknowledged that their power was from Jesus. He fearlessly used this situation as another opportunity to witness for Christ.

Peter and John had been arrested partly because of the commotion that had occurred as a result of their healing a lame man in the temple area. Peter testified that it was by the name of Jesus that the man had been healed (Acts 4:10). He also proclaimed that there was no other way to be saved than through the name of Jesus (Acts 4:12). That was the real purpose for healing the crippled man, and it is the primary reason why God allows Christians to go through times of persecution. As Christians witness for Christ in trying times, and people are saved, or as Christians reach out in trying times, meeting needs and touching lives for the Lord, it is *to illustrate the power of Christ*. Only a short time before, Peter had denied that he was a follower of Christ for fear of losing his life. Now he was boldly proclaiming the gospel of Christ without regard for his life. It was because Peter knew what Paul later expressed was also a desire of his life: "That I may know Him and the power of His resurrection" (Phil. 3:10). Peter knew the power of the Lord's resurrection. That power was greater than any persecution the believers would face.

Another reason why God allows persecution to come upon his followers is that we might *identify with the passion of Christ*. The Bible refers to what Christ did at Calvary as his passion (Acts 1:3). It was because of his love for us, his passion for us, that he endured the suffering of Calvary. Paul said that he not only wanted to know Christ and "the power of His resurrection," but he also wanted to know "the fellowship of His sufferings" (Phil. 3:10). Those in the early church counted it a privilege to suffer shame for his name because it was a way by which they could identify with the passion of Christ. It identified them as being of Christ and for Christ.

After the first arrest and persecution of some of those early apostles and believers in Christ, the governmental authorities had "commanded them not to speak at all nor teach in the name of Jesus" (Acts 4:18). But they continued to do so. Therefore, they were arrested again. When the high priest asked them, "Did we not strictly command you not to teach in this name?" (Acts 5:28), Peter and the other apostles answered and said, "We ought to obey God rather than men" (Acts 5:29). Peter also used the situation as an opportunity to witness again to those unsaved religious authorities. It made them so furious that they wanted to kill the apostles (Acts 5:33). But the wise advice of a pharisee named Gamaliel (Acts 5:34-39) swayed them from committing such an atrocity. They finally decided to have the apostles beaten. The civil authorities also commanded them again not to speak in the name of Jesus, then they let them go (Acts 5:40).

What was the response of the believers after they had been arrested, beaten, and warned not to witness anymore for Christ? The Bible says, "They departed from the presence of the council, rejoicing that they were counted worthy to suffer shame for His name. And daily in the temple, and in every house, they did not cease teaching and preaching Jesus as the Christ" (Acts 5:41-41). Well, "Glory!"

Paul's words to the church at Philippi confirm the possibility that some Christians will experience the divine discipline of differences in persecution. What he said to the Philippian believers also has present day application: "For to you it has been granted on behalf of Christ, not only to believe in Him, but also to suffer for His sake" (Phil. 1:29). We see this possibility of suffering brought out in the other writings of Paul in the New Testament, in the writings of Peter and James, and also in the book of Hebrews. Those early believers counted it a privilege to suffer for their faith in Christ because it was a way they could give back in the manner he had given himself for them. It caused their passion for Jesus to be much stronger, instead of weakened and relinquished as their persecutors had hoped.

The persecution of the first century church did not hinder the spread of the gospel. It actually *enhanced the penetration of the gospel throughout the world*, as Christians on the run continued to reveal who Jesus was and what he had done as they moved into less hostile areas. Those who had hoped to silence the first Christians thought by harassing them, arresting them, and warning them, that would be enough. But the civil authorities did not know the power of Christ. When the basically verbal harassment did not work, arresting, beating, and warning the believers did not stop the spread of the good news of Jesus. The passion of Christ was an inspiration to the believers. Through their own sufferings, they were able to identify with the great love the Lord had for them. So roughing up Christians did not shut them up in their proclaiming Jesus Christ.

The next step was to begin killing Christians. The sixth and seventh chapters of Acts give the account of the implementation of this next level of persecution against Christians. Stephen was the first Christian put to death. This incited "a great persecution against the church which was at Jerusalem" (Acts 8:1). The result was that the church began to scatter. But that was not a sign of defeat. It was a signal to advance.

Acts 8:1 says that the church at Jerusalem "scattered throughout the regions of Judea and Samaria, except the apostles." Did this cause them to flee in fear of their lives to go into hiding? No! The Bible says that "those who were scattered went everywhere preaching the word"

(Acts 8:4). *Acts 8:1 was necessary for Acts 1:8 to be fulfilled.* In Acts 1:8, the Bible records the last words that Jesus spoke before he ascended into heaven: "But you shall receive power when the Holy Spirit has come upon you; and you shall be witnesses to Me in Jerusalem, and in all Judea and Samaria, and to the end of the earth." The persecution that became so intense, beginning with Stephen's death, brought about the fulfillment of Acts 1:8. The church at Jerusalem had such a wonderful, loving fellowship that they just wanted to be together all the time. Persecution caused them to leave the confines and comfort of their local family of faith to proclaim the person of Christ throughout the world. They were scattered abroad, preaching the Word.

How did the early church preach the Word? They simply preached Jesus. That is how Philip infiltrated the person of Christ everywhere he went. He went to Samaria and "preached Christ to them" (Acts 8:5). People were saved, and "there was great joy in that city" (Acts 8:8). Later in his travels, Philip witnessed to an Ethiopian, who was over the queen's treasury. The man happened to be studying the scriptures, so Philip began with the passage the man was studying and "preached Jesus to him" (Acts 8:35). The man got saved. That is what happened everywhere Christians went after the persecution arose over Stephen (Acts 11:19). They preached the Lord Jesus, by testifying to the person of Christ as revealed through his passion and the power of his resurrection. The result was that large numbers of people "believed and turned to the Lord" (Acts 11:21). That is what has happened every time Christians have been persecuted.

> *Persecution caused them to leave the confines and comfort of their local family of faith to proclaim the person of Christ throughout the world.*

What those who persecuted Christians did not realize was that their persecution of believers was the catalyst of releasing the greatest strength and power Christians have possible. The strength and power of Jesus are most revealed to us and through us in our times of difficulty and weakness (2 Cor. 12:9). In times of persecution, Christ is our only source of strength and power. Nobody can snuff out his power, not even our persecutors.

The principle has held true throughout the nineteen hundred years since the first major persecution of Christians occurred and the church scattered, preaching the gospel. In 1949, with the Communist takeover of China, all the Christian missionaries were expelled from the country. At the time, there were about 700,000 Chinese Christians. That number remained constant until 1966 when Mao Zedong and his Red Gang unleashed the Cultural Revolution, and it swept across the country. Churches were closed and confiscated to become schools, government offices or warehouses, or boarded up. Bibles, hymnals, and other Christian literature were burned in the streets. Godly pastors were imprisoned and either put to death or sent to hard labor. Christians were forbidden to worship with the penalty of death if they were caught doing so. The watching world on the outside thought that surely the church would die in China.

As the Cultural Revolution continued for the next ten years, the outside world knew little about the workings and conditions within Communist China. With the death of Mao in 1976, and the arrest of the Gang of Four, the outside world once again got a look inside China as the Bamboo Curtain was slightly lifted. What had happened to the church? Not only had it survived, but it had thrived. The church in China had passed through a baptism of persecution, like that of the first century church, but persecution had not snuffed out the power of Christ and his church. Today there are over eighty million Chinese Christians. Glory to God! Persecution has always resulted in the advance of the gospel, not in its retreat and defeat. The church in China is still persecuted today, but Chinese Christians keep marching on for the cause of Christ, and what a modern day example of bold faith they continue to be for us.

Yes, God does allow divine differences of persecution. He even brings it upon some of us, not as punishment, but as a means by which the power, passion, and person of Christ can be revealed to a world that desperately needs what he can do for them because of what he has done for them. To those on whom God has bestowed the high calling of being persecuted for righteousness' sake, they consider it a reason for rejoicing in their being worthy to suffer shame for his name (Acts 5:41).

DIVINE DIFFERENCES IN PERSONALITY

Divine differences in personality is another aspect of divine differences that can be experienced in any area of life. Is one's style of personality in doing a similar task better than another? Not necessarily! God has made each of us the way we are for a purpose. You are the way you are because that is how God made you and that is how he wants you to be. You may think that God has given more grace to someone else when it comes to the way he has made them, but the Bible says that we are all "wonderfully made" (Ps. 139:14). In the passage where David wrote those words, he also said,

> *For You formed my inward parts; You covered me in my mother's womb. . . . Marvelous are Your works, and that my soul knows very well. My frame was not hidden from You, when I was made in secret, and skillfully wrought in the lowest parts of the earth. Your eyes saw my substance, being yet unformed. And in Your book they all were written, the days fashioned for me, when as yet there were none of them. (Ps. 139:13-16)*

Just think, those divinely inspired words tell us that God already knew what we were going to look like and be like before we were ever born.

In the introduction to the concept of divine differences, the illustration was used of how the temperament of Peter's personality was such that we remember some of his faults more than we do those of the other disciples. Because of his outgoing, outspoken personality, he was the one who usually responded first to the questions and stories the Master Teacher used to illustrate the lessons he was teaching his followers. But we ought to be careful before we get too hard on Peter for his often impetuous and incorrect remarks. It appears that the Lord really wanted and actually expected the disciples to often answer wrongly. It was because the lessons our Lord taught on how to respond to life situations were often contrary to what would be the logical or normal response. Because Peter normally spoke first, he was the one credited with the wrong answer, although most everyone else would have answered the same way. From the reactions to Peter's personality, there are some lessons we can learn that will encourage us to accept our own personality traits.

To a great extent, *your personality influences what people remember about you.* There were so many things that were right about Peter, but one thing that stands out in our minds is that he was the disciple who denied knowing Christ and being one of his followers. Yet all the disciples actually denied the Lord. Matthew 26:56 says that when Christ was arrested in the Garden of Gethsemane, "then all the disciples forsook Him and fled." If they had not been in hiding where no one could find them and confront them, which was not the situation with Peter, the other disciples may have openly denied the Lord too. There was some bravery in Peter at first, which was not shown by the nine disciples who fled, because he did go to the place where the accusers of the Lord had taken him for a trial.

John was the other disciple the Bible refers to in John 18:15 who followed Jesus to the home of the high priest. He was the one who was able to get Peter into the courtyard of the high priest. We have no record that John spoke in defense of Christ during the inquisition at the home of the high priest. So, in reality, John actually denied the Lord. But we remember Peter as the one who denied Christ. Jesus did prophesy that Peter would deny him, but all the others did too. Because of the nature of Peter's personality, he was the one whom the Lord used as an example in his denial of being a follower of Christ. The significance of that will be discussed later in this chapter. But we remember Peter as the one who denied the Lord because his personality made him vulnerable. He was so determined and strong-willed that he was where the other disciples were not on the night that Christ was condemned to die. He was right where it happened.

Your personality also *affects the way people receive you.* Certain kinds of personalities lead to more interaction with and from people than do other kinds of personalities. Sometimes, those who have an opinion about everything need to be corrected. The best way to correct someone is in a way that gets their attention and brings about the desired result. That is how the Lord had to treat Peter. One minute you would find Jesus praising Peter—"Blessed are you, Simon-Bar-Jonah, for flesh and blood has not revealed this to you, but my Father who is in heaven. And I also say to you that you are Peter, and on this rock I will build My church, and the gates of Hades shall not prevail against it" (Matt. 16:17-18), this was after Peter had acknowledged Jesus as "the Christ, the Son of the living God"—but a few verses later, we find Peter taking Jesus aside to tell him to quit saying that he was going to be killed. The Lord's praise then turned to rebuke: "Get behind Me, Satan! You are an offense to Me, for you are not mindful of the things of God, but the things of men" (Matt. 16:23).

Jesus dealt with Peter's personality traits as was appropriate to the situation. Peter was a very likable, loyal, and well-meaning individual. But as his reactions and responses were often overbearing and too impulsive at times, Jesus had to deal with them immediately and firmly on occasion. The reactions you receive from people can tell you a lot about your personality. If you receive strong reactions from people, just make sure that you did not receive such a response because of inconsistency in your Christian life. If you boldly stand for Jesus, you are always going to have those who will be critical of you. Peter had some moments in his life when he just plain blew it! But Jesus knew what Peter had the potential to become, and the Lord's discipline of Peter helped him to reach that potential. You can be assured that the devil had a knowledge of Peter's love for Jesus and the great man of faith and powerful witness he had the potential of becoming. It was to the extent that Satan desired him. Jesus told Peter that "Satan has asked for you" (Luke 22:31). Satan wanted Peter to fall because he might have considered Peter to be the most influential of the disciples. Peter did fall, but he got back up, and he used this time of shame and brokenness in his life to rise to greater heights as a witness for Christ, which was greater than he ever imagined possible.

> *If you boldly stand for Jesus, you are always going to have those who will be critical of you.*

We need all the diverse personalities that are found in churches. If we were all clones who always looked alike, always thought alike, and always acted alike, there would be those who may never be reached for Christ. Having "all things in common" and being "in one accord" does not disallow individual, unique personalities. You will have a more effective witness with some individuals than your peers will have because your personality appeals to them. Why are you able to reach people for Christ whom others have not been able to? It is because you have a personality which *appeals to the people whom you are able to reach*. God has made you the way you are "according to the good pleasure of His will" (Eph. 1:9; Phil. 2:13). He has made you just the way you are because that is how God wants to reveal himself to the world through you.

What a freeing time it is in your life when you can accept the way God has "wonderfully made" (Ps. 139:14) you and you allow him to work through your unique, specially designed personality.

CONCLUSION

Which of the men whom we have examined in this chapter on divine differences was more righteous, more filled with the Holy Spirit, or closer to God? Was it Joshua, Caleb, John, Peter, James, Stephen, or Paul? The Bible says that they were all filled with the Holy Spirit. None was more righteous than any of the others. All had a close walk with the Lord. But why did God choose Joshua over Caleb? Why did God allow James and Stephen to die, but he spared Peter and gave him a longer earthly ministry for Christ? Why did the Lord seem to pick on Peter and make an example of him? Why did John appear to get better treatment on some matters than Peter? An answer to some of those questions or at least an understanding into how the Lord works through divine differences has been given in this chapter. Life is full of such difficult questions. Why is one child physically handicapped and another athletically gifted? Why do some people die before reaching their potential? Why do some people, who are not any more qualified, get that better position or job you wanted? Those are questions we cannot completely answer in this earthly life because we do not see all that God sees, and we do not know all that God knows. It is the nature of divine differences.

At the beginning of this chapter, the comment was made that if you are on what appears to be the low side of divine differences, it is not something to be dejected about. It is something to rejoice about. We have seen how one's position in life may change at any time. Your standing true to the Lord during difficult times may be to the advantage of your heirs in making it possible for them to enjoy years of peace and prosperity. Your being the one who always seems to be getting corrected for your mistakes or misbehavior may be your ladder to success as you grow older and wiser. Whatever your station in life, you can be assured that God is working all things for your good.

If God has selected you to be on the down side of divine differences in position, persecution, or personality, it tells you some positive and encouraging things about yourself. It especially tells you how highly God thinks about you. In divine differences, the Lord wants your reactions and responses to glorify Christ. If he is allowing you to be on what appears to be the unfair side of divine differences, it is because the Lord knows that he can count on you. For example, if you are going through divine differences in persecution, the Lord knows that you will be strong and courageous in remaining a witness for Christ.

If you feel that God is divinely disciplining you through divine differences, then accept it and allow God to work in you for his good pleasure. He will help you use disappointment, suffering, and dismay in a way that will strengthen your faith in Christ and glorify him through your life. God has promised that he will never leave us or forsake us and that all things work together for good. If you are experiencing the down side of divine differences—that suffering, unfair side—then continue to be faithful, obedient, and trustworthy. Let others see Jesus in you. Rejoice because God thinks so highly of you. And remember, a day of reward is coming. You may see some of it in this earthly life, but, know for certain, the fruition of it will ultimately take place in your true homeland, which is your heavenly country (Heb. 11:13-16).

8: DIVINE DIFFICULTY

"FOR CHRIST'S SAKE"

Divine Difficulty: *A season of time when life is difficult and there is really nothing you can do other than keep at it and keep asking God to give you the strength to endure it.*

I desired to get a seminary degree years before I was able to pursue such a degree. At the age of thirty-one, I accepted a ministerial staff position at a church that was located twenty miles from a college campus where a seminary had extension classes on Mondays. For four years I took two to three seminary classes on Mondays. Eventually, on campus course work was necessary to earn a master of divinity degree, which would require moving several hundred miles away to finish the degree. After I had gone as far in this program as I could, the "still, small voice" of the Holy Spirit, which often speaks much louder than audible words, began prompting me to preach. As I felt directed by the Lord, I resigned my church position and enrolled at a seminary which was located where I had recently moved to serve on the ministerial staff at a church in my hometown of Memphis, Tennessee.

Although the Monday program would have taken about seven years to get my seminary degree, I had adjusted well to classes only one day a week with six days of study time before the next class. But when I entered seminary full time, it was a major adjustment for this thirty-six-year-old married man with two children. I had four classes, which included Greek. I would come home after classes and study until dinner. Then I would study more after supper. I often had to get up early in the morning for more studying before I took our kids to pre-school. I would drop them off at school, head to seminary, and the process would start again. I was also serving in a part time capacity as director of singles at my home church. I was trying to be a good husband and daddy within this schedule. By the grace and strength of God I made it through that first term. Eventually, it was not quite as difficult as I got more adjusted to this routine. Praise the Lord, my wife and children endured it too!

I must admit, though, that during that first term of full-time seminary, I felt like quitting Tuesday through Thursday. When classes were over on Friday, I could take heart in that another week was over. I would get motivated again over the weekend. My wife and I were also having to deal with the financial burden of our income having been reduced by almost 90 percent.

I knew the Lord had led me to take this route in my life. I knew that I was not going to quit and that the Lord was going to help us make it through. But that did not keep it from being one of the most difficult times of our lives. It was a time when my wife and I experienced the divine discipline of *divine difficulty*. Those three years of full-time seminary, especially the first year, were probably the most difficult of our lives, but they were among the best years of our lives. What a joy and thrill it was for me when my wife and three children (the Lord blessed us with another child during this time) got to see their husband and daddy graduate and receive the master of divinity degree with honors. At Mid-America Baptist Theological Seminary, they give the wives of the graduates a P.H.T. (Putting Husband Through) degree. My wife certainly earned it. We can both look back now at that time of divine difficulty and see how God used it in our lives. It was a time of growing us and maturing us in our faith as nothing else had up to that point in our lives.

Life is going to be difficult, at times. You can really do nothing about it other than to keep at it and to keep asking God to give you the strength to endure it. You may feel that the illustration I have given of a time of divine difficulty in my life is nothing compared to what you have gone through or are presently going through. Well, my friend, I can tell you that you can endure it and you can become better because of it. I know it from experience, but that is not what I am basing my advice upon. I have had other difficult times in my life that are equal to or worse than my seminary years. You see, it is an expectation of the Christian life. You can expect difficulties in your life, but you can endure them. How do I know this to be so? It comes from the source where I learned how to get through divine difficulty. In this chapter we are going to look at what the Bible says about divine difficulty and examine the life of one who suffered more for Christ's sake than any other personality in the Bible. Our example is Paul. The Bible gives an overview of God's purpose for divine difficulty in 2 Corinthians 4:7-15:

> *But we have this treasure in earthen vessels, that the excellence of the power may be of God and not of us. We are hard pressed on every side, yet not crushed; we are perplexed, but not in despair; persecuted, but not forsaken; struck down, but not destroyed—always carrying about in the body the dying of the Lord Jesus, that the life of Jesus also may be manifested in our body. For we who live are always delivered to death for Jesus' sake, that the life of Jesus also may be manifested in our mortal flesh. So then death is working in us, but life in you. And since we have the same spirit of faith, according to what is written, "I believed and therefore I spoke," we also believe and therefore speak, knowing that He who raised up the Lord Jesus will also raise us up with Jesus, and will present us with you. For all things are for your sakes, that grace, having spread through the many, may cause thanksgiving to abound to the glory of God.*

> *"There is no development of Christ-likeness in a person's life apart from suffering."*

In the introduction to this book, the statement was made that "there is no development of Christ-likeness in a person's life apart from suffering. Difficulties are necessary occurrences in the growth and development of our Christian lives." We receive positive spiritual benefits from divine difficulty. Difficulties are meant to help us grow and mature into the people of faith God wants us to be. Paul experienced great difficulty throughout his life as a witness for Christ, yet it never seemed to slow him down. His difficulties were a springboard to greater rejoicing in his life. From the passage in 2 Corinthians 4, Paul gives three reasons for divine difficulty:

that the power of Christ may stay upon us; that the presence of Christ may be strong in us; and that the person of Christ may be seen through us.

That the Power of Christ May Stay Upon Us

Paul gives a first reason why God sends divine difficulty upon us in verse seven of 2 Corinthians 4. He says it is "that the excellency of the power may be of God and not of us." Paul referred to this possibility as "treasure in earthen vessels" (1 Cor. 4:7). Paul had attained many worldly accomplishments in his life, but he counted all things loss compared to "the excellence of the knowledge of Christ Jesus my Lord, for whom I have suffered the loss of all things, and count them as rubbish, that I may gain Christ" (Phil. 3:7-8). Paul was sold out and surrendered to Jesus. He wanted Christ to be magnified in his life (Phil. 1:20). He knew that could only happen in his life with Jesus as his continual source of power. Paul learned that it was during his times of difficulty when he sensed the greatest flow of power. The Lord had confirmed this to him when he told Paul, "My grace is sufficient for you, for My strength is made perfect in weakness" (2 Cor. 12:9). So Paul's approach to his difficulties was this: "Most gladly I will rather boast in my infirmities, that the power of Christ may rest upon me. Therefore I take pleasure in infirmities, in reproaches, in needs, in persecutions, in distresses, for Christ's sake. For when I am weak, then I am strong" (2 Cor. 12:9-10).

We learn from Paul that divine difficulty is sent into our lives so *that the power of Christ may stay upon us.* I mentioned in chapter one that I heard the late Jerry Falwell make this statement at a conference in 1986: "If I have two good days back to back, my prayer life suffers." He made that statement while preaching a sermon he titled, "Christians in a Pressure Cooker." He was encouraging Christians on how to deal with the pressures of life. Dr. Falwell went on to explain his statement by acknowledging that when things are always going our way, we tend to get self-sufficient, and we do not lean on God and follow his guidance as we should. So God sends difficulties into our lives *to keep us dependent on him.*

As we trust God to see us through the storms of life, we develop a strong, mature faith that shows us peace in the midst of the storm as he sees us through time after time. The Bible says that God will keep him in perfect peace whose mind is stayed on the Lord (Isa. 26:3). As we stay upon the Lord during difficult times, because he is the one we are dependent upon in our difficulties, the power of Christ will stay upon us, and he will be our strength to help us endure.

We are dependent upon the Lord the most when we have our greatest need of him. That comes in our times of difficulty. We need to have fellowship with Christ all the time, and how sweet and precious those times are with him when we are not burdened with pressing needs in our lives. But the Bible says that it is in our times of pressure and difficulties when the power of Christ is manifested the most.

Divine difficulty not only keeps us dependent on the Lord, but it *gets us dedicated to him*. The Bible is full of God's promises to us, but they do come with conditions. his promises are conditional upon our obedience. God says, "Obey My voice, and I will be your God, and you shall be My people. And walk in all the ways that I have commanded you, that it may be well with you" (Jer. 7:23). Of course, when you disobey God, he will eventually bring difficulties upon you to get your attention. He does not have to bring the difficulties upon us much of the time because the natural result of living an unfaithful Christian life is one difficulty after another.

When you are living a life of obedience to the Lord, he will allow enough difficulties in your life to keep you from being too self-sufficient. That keeps you dependent on him and dedicated to him. The more dependent you are upon someone, the more dedicated you will be to that person. Our dedication to God comes not only because we depend upon him, but out of our love for him. It is only natural for the Christian. When the one you are dependent on has an eternal love for you and does what he does in your life out of love for you, then you want to be dedicated to him. We love because he first loved us (1 John 4:19).

Paul was dedicated to God because of love. After he was saved, it became the compelling factor behind the purpose for his life as a minister of the gospel. He brought this out when he said, "For we do not preach ourselves, but Christ Jesus the Lord, and ourselves your bondservants for Jesus' sake. For it is the God who commanded light to shine out of darkness, who has shone in our hearts to give the light of the knowledge of the glory of God in the face of Jesus Christ" (2 Cor. 4:5-6).

When we are dependent on the Lord and dedicated to the Lord out of love for him, that is when we are effective disciples of Christ. Divine difficulty comes into our lives *to make us disciples for Him.* Oswald Chambers said, "God will never shield you from any of the requirements of a son or daughter of His."[11] Paul wrote that Christians could expect difficulty in some way at various times in their lives. Peter also confirmed this fact: "Beloved, do not think it strange concerning the fiery trial which is to try you, as though some strange thing happened to you" (1 Pet. 4:12). Yes, Christian, "to you it has been granted on behalf of Christ, not only to believe in Him, but also to suffer for His sake (Phil. 1:29), for "all who desire to live godly in Christ Jesus will suffer persecution" (2 Tim. 3:12). Most of us will probably not have to suffer that kind of difficulty, but we may. You can be assured that there will be difficulties in the Christian life. They are requirements for sons and daughters of God.

How should you react to divine difficulty? Oswald Chambers gave good advice: "Rise to the occasion; do the thing. It does not matter how it hurts as long as it gives God the chance to manifest Himself in your mortal flesh."[12] In divine difficulty, just keep on keeping on. Keep on doing what you ought to be doing consistently as a Christian, and the power of Christ will stay upon you. Then, like Paul, you will have treasure in your earthen vessel because you will have the excellency of the power of God working in you.

THAT THE PRESENCE OF CHRIST MAY BE STRONG IN US

A second purpose of divine difficulty is *that the presence of Christ may be strong in us.* When the power of Christ stays upon you, its natural result should be that the presence of Christ will be strong in you. Paul referred to this element of divine difficulty as "always carrying about in the body the dying of the Lord Jesus, that the life of Jesus also may be manifested in our body" (2 Cor. 4:10). When I am physically fit, I know it, because my body tells me so. I can jog three or four miles and feel great afterwards, even the day after. But after time off periods from exercise, it is especially evident the day or two after I have jogged that

11. Chambers, *My Utmost for His Highest*, 98.
12. Ibid.

physical fitness is not manifested in my body. I have aches and pains that I did not think were possible.

God has to keep us spiritually fit or we will get out of shape. Periods of divine difficulty cause us to get back in spiritual shape, especially if we have slacked off during exceptional periods of "divine delight" and "divine desire" where everything just seems to go your way. When you are in spiritual shape, you know it! You sense and feel the power of Christ upon you, and you know the presence of Christ is strong within you. The more you experience divine difficulty, the greater will be the power of Christ upon you and the stronger will be the presence of Christ within you, if you are exercised by divine difficulty.

How are you exercised by divine difficulty so that the presence of Christ is strong within you? Well, God has to strain us and stretch us in order to strengthen us. An athlete in training goes through a process of intentionally straining and stretching his muscles. When done at the right limit and right pace, his muscles will become stronger. He will become better in the sport and activity for which he is training. There are times, though, when a muscle, bone, tendon, or ligament is overstrained or overstretched. The result is a stifling injury that temporarily or permanently puts the athlete out of competition. The key in training is to strain and stretch the muscles and supporting parts so that they will get stronger and will be strong enough to endure the competition without a breakdown.

> *God spiritually strains your faith in order to stretch your faith so that you may become strong in the faith.*

It is the same way in the spiritual life. God spiritually strains your faith in order to stretch your faith so that you may become strong in the faith. As you have to deal with a difficulty, and it is physically, mentally, emotionally, and spiritually demanding, remember, that is when the power of Christ is strong upon you. As the difficulty strains you, and you depend on the help and guidance of the Lord to see you through, when you have passed through the storm your faith will have been stretched. Through the Lord showing you the way through the storm, when a similar difficulty comes again, you will know how to deal with it.

That is basically what happens to the body as you increase your exercise load. Eventually, the body adjusts to the greater demand on it so that it can endure a workout or a contest without a breakdown. Your body gets stronger as you forcibly but controllably stretch and strain it. You can be assured that as God strains you and stretches you through divine difficulty, he will do so at a controlled pace. He knows the right limit and pace at which to exercise you to a greater spiritual strength.

Oswald Chambers said, "The strain is the strength. If there is no strain, there is no strength. Are you asking God to give you life and liberty and joy? He cannot, unless you will accept the strain. Immediately you face the strain, you will get the strength."[13] To manifest the life of Jesus in your body, you must accept the strain that is necessary to stretch your faith, trust, and commitment to the Lord. If you allow divine difficulty to exercise you, as you experience difficulties, instead of spending yourself out physically so that you become exhausted, discouraged, depressed, and defeated, you will exert yourself physically and spiritually with strength that is sufficient for the moment because the presence of Christ is strong within you.

Another quote from Oswald Chambers is a challenging summary of this second purpose of divine difficulty: When the difficulty comes, "may God not find the whine in us any more, but may he find us full of spiritual pluck and athleticism, ready to face anything He brings."[14] When divine difficulty has exercised you to that extent, you will be able to identify with these words of Paul: "We are hard pressed on every side, yet not crushed; we are perplexed, but not in despair; persecuted, but not forsaken; struck down, but not destroyed—always carrying about in the body the dying of the Lord Jesus, that the life of Jesus also may be manifested in our body" (2 Cor. 4:8-10).

THAT THE PERSON OF CHRIST MAY BE SEEN THROUGH US

One other purpose of divine difficulty is ultimately what God is desiring to do in each of our lives. It is the main reason we are left on this earth after we get saved. This reason is given in verse eleven of 2 Corinthians 4: "that the life of Jesus also may be manifested in our

---

13. Chambers, 157.
14. Chambers, 98.

mortal flesh." Not only does divine difficulty come into our lives that the power of Christ may stay upon us and that the presence of Christ may be strong in us, but its supreme purpose is *that the person of Christ may be seen through us.*

Flesh is that part of the body that other people see. When people look at you, what do they see? Actually, who do they see? If you are a Christian, Paul's words indicate that people should not only see you when they look at you. They should also see the evidence that Jesus is living in you. As one of the great hymns of the faith imparts, "let others see Jesus in you."

Jesus emphasized that what people see on the outside identifies who you are and whose you are. He said, "Let you light so shine before men, that they may see your good works and glorify your Father in heaven" (Matt. 5:16). When you are in Christ and his presence is strong within you, the person of Christ is going to be seen through you. Jesus reinforced the proverb that says, "as a man thinks in his heart, so is he" (Prov. 23:7), when the Lord stated, "But the things which proceed out of the mouth come from the heart" (Matt. 15:18). As people see who you are and whose you are by what you say and do, Christ will either be seen through you or he will not be seen through you. Do others see Jesus in you?

If others do not see Jesus in you, then you need to have a heart check-up. As you think in your heart, so are you. Are you truly in Christ? Have you really given your heart to the Lord? Are you born again? Friend, you must be saved to have the presence of Christ in you (Rom. 10:9-10; John 14:15-17). If you know that you know that you know that you know you are saved, yet you do not sense the presence of Christ is strong within you, then you have an obstruction to the spiritual flow of power available to you. As we are dealing in this book with God's discipline for the purpose of maturing sincere, committed Christians, not with his discipline as punishment given to carnal, disobedient Christians, the obstruction to the spiritual power flow in your life could simply be that things are going too well for you. It was mentioned earlier in the chapter that when things are going our way, we tend to get too self-sufficient. We do not lean on God and follow his guidance as we should. God allows difficulties to come so that we will stay dependent upon him, but that is where the power of Christ stays upon us. If divine discipline exercises us, then the presence of Christ will be strong in us. The result is that what is on the inside, what is from the heart, will proceed out of us. The person of Christ will then be seen through us. As one gospel singer used to express several times during a concert, when he just could not contain himself any longer, he would say, "Excuse me for a moment— Well, glory!" The result of divine difficulty puts you on shouting ground.

The aim of life for the Christian is "that the life of Jesus also may be manifested in our mortal flesh" (2 Cor. 4:11). Divine difficulty is an opportunity for Christ to be seen and lived out through your life. How should you face and endure the divine discipline of difficulty so that the person of Christ is seen through you? First, go to God. Where we go in times of trials and difficulties proves where the source of power is in our lives. In difficult times, make God your first choice, not your last desperate resort to which you turn. He knows all the difficulties, and he will solve and dissolve them before us, if we will depend upon him to do so. Bear in mind, too, that the bigger and greater the difficulty, the greater Christ will be manifested in your mortal flesh as you draw from his supernatural power.

> *Where we go in times of trials and difficulties proves where the source of power is in our lives.*

Not only should you go to God in your difficulties, but go with God. To go with God is to go the second mile. During the earthly ministry of Christ, the Roman law allowed a Roman soldier the authority to make a Jewish male carry the soldier's gear for one mile. In the Sermon on the Mount, Jesus said that if you were forced to go one mile, offer to go the second mile as an act of grace (Matt. 5:41). To go the second mile is to do more than your duty. The second mile is where the person of Christ is seen most clearly through you. You see, we live in a day when people do not expect the extra mile because they are not willing to go it themselves. Instead of the "Golden Rule," most of society now seems to live by the "withholden" rule—don't do for others what they don't do for you.

To be with God, though, is to go the extra mile. It is to be different, but a positive difference from most everybody else. Again, I quote

Oswald Chambers because he made a profound statement about going the second mile:

> *To go the second mile means always do your duty, and a great deal more than your duty, in a spirit of loving devotion that does not even know you have done it. If you are a saint the Lord will tax your walking capacity to the limit. The supreme difficulty is to go the second mile with God, because no one understands why you are being such a fool.* "[15]

That is, a fool for Christ (1 Cor. 4:10). As you go with God during divine difficulty, he takes you beyond the first mile, the expected mile. For as you go with God time and time again through difficulties, the second mile eventually becomes second nature for you. It is where Christ is magnified the most through you. Yes, there will be those who will think that you are a fool, but the process will also reproduce some who will join you as "fools for Christ's sake." That is what it is all about.

As you go to God in your difficulties and you go with God through those difficulties, you then have reached a point where you are going for God. Paul treasured his times of difficulties because he knew they came for Christ's sake. The person of Jesus was seen through Paul as he kept pressing on through one difficulty after another. As a result, other Christians were encouraged by his example and converts were added to the faith. That was why he kept pressing on. It caused "thanksgiving to abound to the glory of God" (2 Cor. 4:15).

> *If your idea of the Christian life is that your problems and worries are over when you get saved, or that you are weak in your faith if you have great difficulties, then you are in for a big shock.*

CONCLUSION

If your idea of the Christian life is that your problems and worries are over when you get saved, or that you are weak in your faith if you

---

15. Harry Verploegh, ed., *Oswald Chambers: The Best From All His Books* (Nashville: Oliver-Nelson, 1987), 96.

have great difficulties, then you are in for a big shock. But if you have read all the preceding pages of this book, you are well aware that trials and difficulties are actually expectations of the Christian life.

For many years of my Christian life, I assumed that all the difficulties which came my way were because God was punishing me for something or it was because the devil was attacking me. Some of the time that was the case. But God gets the blame or credit for a lot of things in which he had no influence. For example, I know of some "married but not to each other" couples who claimed that God had led them to each other, so they either separated or divorced their previous mates. God would never lead in such a way. He should not be given credit or blame for such affairs.

Even the devil gets the credit or blame in such manner. Comedian Flip Wilson had a trademark saying that he used in some of his comedy sketches years ago: "The devil made me do it!" When things go awry in the lives of many people, they want to blame it on the devil as the one who made them do it or who caused it to happen. But there are some bad and difficult situations that the devil did not cause which come into the lives of people. Many of our difficulties are brought on simply because of the result of our own poor decisions and actions. So our difficulties may be the result of God's punishment for disobedience, because of the devil's attacks in his desire to see Christians get depressed and discouraged, or because of our own making.

There are, though, difficulties which God brings upon us or allows us to encounter to keep us dependent on him and dedicated to him so that we will be dynamic disciples for him. If you are a child of God, there will be difficulties to face. But as you stay dependent on God and dedicated to him, the power of Christ stays upon you. As the power of Christ stays upon you, the presence of Christ will become stronger in you. Divine difficulty strains you and stretches you, but it also strengthens you, for when you are weak, that is when the life of Jesus develops in you as he becomes your strength. When the presence of Christ is strong in you, you will shine for him and not whine to him. The Christ on your inside will overflow to your outside, and the person of Christ will be seen through you. Where Christ is, the result will always be love, grace, mercy, salvation, joy, and peace.

When do you know that divine difficulty has exercised you for its intended purpose? Divine difficulty is complete in its intent when it produces sons and daughters with a strong, family resemblance to their Father, as manifested through his only begotten Son being seen through them, who are reproducing more sons and daughters with an undeniable kinship and likeness to Christ.

9: Divine

Disappointment

"All Forsook Me but the Lord"

Divine Disappointment: A situation God allows for the purpose of getting our affections and focus off anyone or anything that has become preeminent above Christ in our lives.

Has someone you put on a pedestal, whom you may have looked up to as a spiritual hero, ever come crumbling down off that pedestal, in your eyes? Has someone whom you considered to be a friend ever stabbed you in your back by a critical comment they made about you that eventually got back to you through the rumor mill? Have you ever trusted someone to do something and they failed to do it? Those questions are examples of the ways by which we experience the divine discipline of divine disappointment.

Disappointment comes when your expectations have not been fulfilled. In most cases, disappointment is the result of someone else blowing it, but God sometimes allows you to be a disappointment to someone else. In this chapter, both of those aspects of divine disappointment will be examined. Paul will again be our biblical example because he was one who experienced divine disappointment. His writings to Timothy, as recorded in 2 Timothy 4:9-18, give us an insight into God's purposes for divine disappointment:

Be diligent to come to me quickly; for Demas has forsaken me, having loved this present world, and has departed for Thessalonica—Crescens for Galatia, Titus for Dalmatia. Only Luke is with me. Get Mark and bring him with you, for he is useful to me for ministry. And Tychicus I have sent to Ephesus. Bring the cloak that I left with Carpus at Troas when you come—and the books, especially the parchments. Alexander the coppersmith did me much harm. May the Lord repay him according to his works. You also must beware of him, for he has greatly resisted our words. At my first defense no one stood with me, but all forsook me. May it not be charged against them.

But the Lord stood with me and strengthened me, so that the message might be preached fully through me, and that all the Gentiles might hear. And I was delivered out of the mouth of the lion. And the Lord will deliver me from every evil work and preserve me for His heavenly kingdom. To Him be glory forever and ever. Amen!

In this passage, Paul specifically makes reference to two individuals who had disappointed him. Demas, evidently, was a believer. In Paul's epistle to the Colossians, he sends them greetings from Demas: "Luke the beloved physician and Demas greet you" (Col. 4:14). In his epistle to Philemon, Paul sends greetings from Demas and refers to him, along with several others, as "my fellow laborers" (Philem. 24). So Demas had been a traveling companion and fellow laborer in the ministry with Paul. But there came a time when Paul had to say, "Demas has forsaken me, having loved this present world" (2 Tim. 4:9). Most likely, Demas had left Paul, rather than face the same possible fate that awaited Paul in his imprisonment which eventually resulted in his execution.

The other individual who disappointed Paul was Alexander the coppersmith. He probably was not a true believer in Christ. Paul said that Alexander did him "much harm" and "greatly resisted our words." Paul warned Timothy to "beware of him" (2 Tim. 4:14-15). If Alexander was a believer, he would have been like those Paul described in Philippians 1:15-16: "Some indeed preach Christ even from envy and strife, and some also from good will: the former preach Christ from selfish ambition, not sincerely, supposing to add affliction to my chains."

As a Christian, you expect resistance from those who are not of the faith, but how greatly disappointing it is when you encounter opposition from within the family of faith. It is especially disappointing when someone, who has served side by side with you in the ministry, falls back or completely falls out in their calling as a minister of the gospel, as apparently was the case with Demas.

It is encouraging, though, that Paul mentioned the need of Mark to come to him. Paul said, "He is useful to me for ministry" (2 Tim. 4:11). Mark had greatly disappointed Paul at one time, to the extent that it split up Paul and Barnabas as a missionary team. Mark had departed from them on a previous mission (Acts 13:13). When Barnabas wanted Mark to accompany them on another mission, "Paul insisted that they should not take with them the one who had departed from them in Pamhylia, and had not gone with them to the work" (Acts 15:38). The contention between Paul and Barnabas over the matter "became so sharp that they parted from one another" (Acts 15:39). As Paul was writing to Timothy in the passage from 2 Timothy 4, it was years later. Mark was no longer a disappointment to Paul. This is encouraging because it lets us know that although divine disappointment comes into our lives, it can be overcome and work for the good of all concerned. The one who had greatly disappointed Paul at one time was now a blessing to him. Mark was now needed by Paul.

> *As a Christian, you expect resistance from those who are not of the faith, but how greatly disappointing it is when you encounter opposition from within the family of faith.*

At the time of the writing of 2 Timothy, Paul did have those who were remaining faithful to him and were supportive of him, but only Luke was present with Paul. Demas had deserted him, Titus and Crescens had gone elsewhere, most likely, for ministry reasons, and Paul acknowledged that he had sent Tychicus on a mission. He was lonely. Paul had gone through a difficult period when he felt as though "all forsook me" (2 Tim. 4:16). All of us have probably had times in our lives when we felt as though "all forsook me." You may have felt or feel right now that your family and your closest friends have not been as supportive or understanding on a matter as you think they should have been. Seldom, if ever, would that really be the case with your family and friends. Such thoughts tend to occur when you are sick or have been under great physical strain and stress, resulting in your tired body and mind going haywire. Usually, all that is needed is a good night of sleep or a few days of rest and relaxation. There are benefits, though, of being so disappointed that you feel "all forsook me," even if factually that is not the case.

People are going to disappoint you on occasion, and it may even be more often than you expect it to happen. But if you respond properly to the disappointments others bring upon you, the effect is divinely beneficial. God is usually not the main influence which causes others to do what are disappointing things to you. We Christians are seeking to mind the things of the Spirit (Rom. 8:5), but as we live in a world of people who predominantly are not Christians, most of the people in the world around us are setting their minds on the things of the flesh and living according to the flesh. This battle between the "flesh" and the "Spirit" is one that even Christians have to face every day. As Christians give in to fleshly desires, that is when those we trust the most do things that disappoint us.

There are times, too, when God is the main influence in allowing others to disappoint us or allowing us to be a disappointment to others. But he has positive reasons for doing it. Whether God has directly allowed disappointments to come into your life or human nature has been the primary source of your disappointments, the term, "divine disappointment," will be used for both because your disappointments can result in divine benefits, if you will allow them to exercise you spiritually. Otherwise, the disappointments you experience will rob you of joy and peace in your life. From Paul's life, there are at least three benefits that divine disappointment can bring into your life: that Christ may be preeminent in your life; to keep you from being puffed up with pride; and that you may point others to Christ.

THAT CHRIST MAY BE PREEMINENT IN YOUR LIFE

As Paul was writing to Timothy from his confinement in Rome, he expressed disappointment. At this difficult and lonely time in his life, it seemed to Paul as though "all forsook me." A few words later, though, we find one of the purposes of divine disappointment: "But the Lord stood with me and strengthened me" (2 Tim. 4:17). All forsook Paul, but the Lord. Paul knew that the Lord was the one person in whom he could completely trust. God desires for our lives what is best for us, and he wants to give us what is best for us. But, at times, we look to other sources as the primary source for our needs. There is no one else who can satisfy our needs as God, so he will allow those other sources to which we turn to disappoint us. A purpose of divine disappointment is to get you to the point *that Christ is preeminent in your life.*

Paul wrote to the Christians at Colossae that Christ was to be first and foremost in their lives so "that in all things He may have the preeminence" (Col. 1:18). Jesus said that the greatest commandment is to "love the Lord your God with all your heart, with all your soul, and with all your mind" (Matt. 22:37). Jesus acknowledged that to believe in God, you must believe in his Son (John 14:1). He also said that the only way to God is through the Son (John 14:6). The Lord God the Father is glorified in the Lord Jesus, his Son (John 14:13). Jesus said, "He who has my commandments and keeps them, it is he who loves Me. And he who loves Me will be loved by My Father, and I will love him and manifest Myself to him" (John 14:21). So to love the Lord God with all your heart, soul, and mind, is to make Christ preeminent in your life.

What keeps Jesus from being preeminent in your life? It is when somebody or something receives more attention and priority in your life other than the Lord. When that is the case, you have essentially made that person your lord or that thing your idol. No human can live up to such a high expectation on your part. A thing that becomes your idol will eventually be replaced as your main focus of attention by some other thing that comes along and grabs your interest. Some people, though, do become fanatical over one thing, and they cannot get over it, and their whole life seems to evolve around it. Things such as snow skiing, water skiing, fishing, hunting, golf, your favorite sports team, or your hobby are just a few examples. They are things that even Christians support, participate in, and give priority to, especially when they have to choose between being faithful to church services and programs or "doing their thing."

When a thing becomes idol worship, God will usually remove the thing temporarily or permanently from your life until you get your spiritual priorities right. When a person becomes an idol or lord in your life, get ready for the pedestal that is going to come crashing down at your feet. No human being can be and do in your life what only Christ can. You cannot place unreal expectations on people that they can never live up to. Yet, we do, and we are going to be disappointed. Whether God has seen to it that the disappointment comes or it is the natural effect of an unnatural expectation, it will eventually come. There are two usual side effects that you will experience in your life when someone has disappointed you: *disillusionment* and *distrust*.

God allows us to be disappointed so that we will be disillusioned. But the *disillusionment* which comes from God is to bring us back to reality where we see people as they really are, not what we unrealistically expect them to be. It is to divinely exercise us so that we will not react to those who disappoint us by having critical, cutting, and callous things to say about them or to them. It is to keep us from becoming cold, bitter, resentful, and revengeful. Much of the ugliness and cruelty in life, which we even see among Christians, is because of the false illusions we dream up. We have our idea of what someone ought to be. As long as they live up to our expectation, everything is just fine. But when someone does not live up to our expectation, we can get hateful, hurtful, and bitter in the resulting disillusionment and distrust. Why? Because if we love a human being more than we love God, or we expect from someone what only God is capable of accomplishing, then we are actually demanding perfection. Since no human can fulfill an expectation of perfection, we become disillusioned because we have built our view of others on false ideas.

> *That is why God allows you to be disillusioned, sometimes, with those people you look up to the most.*

Only one person who ever walked on this earth was perfect—Jesus. That is why God allows you to be disillusioned, sometimes, with those people you look up to the most. If you put anyone or anything higher and with more prominence in your life than Jesus, you are guilty of idol worship. Normally, when this happens in the life of a sincere Christian, he is not even aware of it. It is a "blind spot" in the person's life he does not realize has developed. So God allows disappointment to come. It is to disillusion you back to reality. It is so that you will realize that people and things can be harmful when they are put on a level with God. Christ is to be preeminent in your life. When your spiritual priorities are right, everything else will be viewed in its proper perspective, including people and things.

As divine disappointment gets you disillusioned to the point that you do not have false illusions and expectations, you will also learn to *distrust* others. But it will be just the right, proper level of distrust. You see, the resulting distrust that you have in someone who has disappointed you either works according to God's purpose or to your detriment. God wants to get you to the point that you trust in him with all your heart (Prov. 3:5). To trust him with all your heart is to trust him supremely above all others and all else. Distrust of others works for your good if it is within the perspective that you do not trust anyone's word over the Lord's. That is the proper level of distrust you are to learn from divine disappointment. It is not to get so distrusting that you are paranoid of others, always on the lookout for someone to take advantage of you, so that you are not trusting of anyone. Yes, people will fail you, at times, but Jesus never fails. He does influence your life through other people. You just need to be distrusting of others to the point that you will not trust them more than the Lord. Keep Christ preeminent in your life.

As God does speak through others to influence and guide you, you need to be aware of and alert to some characteristics that should be evident in those who are influences in your life. If you are being highly influenced by someone's words, be sure that their words are in agreement with the sure words of God's Word. It also must be evident that the person of influence in your life is Spirit filled and Spirit led. How do you know if someone is Spirit filled and Spirit led? The Bible tells us so (Ps. 119:105). What they say will be confirmed through God's Word and it will never contradict the Bible. Another sign of one who is Spirit filled and Spirit led is that "those who live according to the flesh set their minds on the things of the flesh, but those who live according to the Spirit, the things of the Spirit" (Rom. 8:5).

You first need to make sure that you are walking in the Spirit, then your spirit will bear witness with those who are walking in the Spirit. To some people, that may sound like a spiritually arrogant statement. It is not meant to be offensive. It is a truth of the Word of God. It is said to caution you, because if you are not Spirit controlled, you can be influenced and led by someone who appears to you to be Spirit minded, but they really are not. They look genuine and act like the real thing, but inwardly they are in the flesh. You do not know it because the same is actually true of your life. When what is on the inside comes out, you are in for a big dose of disillusionment and distrust—divine disappointment. Make sure that you are walking in the Spirit. Trust God supremely and completely. Only trust others in their influence and leadership upon your life by their guidance and actions being confirmed in the Bible and in your spirit. Keep Christ preeminent in your life.

TO KEEP YOU FROM BEING PUFFED UP WITH PRIDE

In the introduction to this chapter, it was said that, in most cases, divine disappointment comes when someone has disappointed you. But God sometimes allows you to be a disappointment to others. The Lord will allow something you do or something that you do not do to disappoint someone, especially when they have placed you on a pedestal. A few years ago, one dear lady felt that her pastor could do no wrong. In her eyes, he was a perfect man. She believed everything he said. In her opinion, every way he suggested that something should be done when it came to spiritual matters was the only way it could be done. In her mind, she had built an image that her pastor and no other human being could ever live up to. But something happened where her pastor did not live up to her unreal expectations, and he came crumbling off the pedestal she had placed him on. What caused that pastor to fall in her eyes was not something he had done that was immoral, shocking, or unusual. It was simply a normal human being reacting to a circumstance differently than another human being wanted him to react.

As I was aware of that particular situation, I would not have reacted to the matter which concerned the woman the way the pastor reacted. I believe that he made a mistake. But we all make mistakes, and sometimes we do not make the right decisions. Yes, even pastors! Anyway, God used the incident to disillusion a dear Christian lady back to reality so that her pastor would not be expected to live up to a standard only Jesus could live up to.

The ordeal was of benefit to the woman and her pastor. People were able to see that although he was a godly man, he was also human and capable of making mistakes. It took pressure off him from having to be what he could never be—a man with no faults, who was always right. It made the woman a stronger Christian with Jesus preeminent in her life and her only model of perfection. For many years God used the same pastor and the same lady in the same church, where they both effectively won people to Christ and helped others to grow in their walk with the Lord. God allowed divine disappointment to come to that woman so that Christ would be preeminent in her life.

Besides being relieved from pressure to be perfect, there is another positive effect such a situation can have on a spiritual leader. God will allow you and me to be a disappointment to others because of the effect it needs to have on our egos. When others begin to think too highly of us, as hard as we say we try to keep from it, we have a tendency to get big-headed. Paul called it getting "puffed up" (1 Cor. 4:6, 18-19; 8:1-2; Col. 2:18). God may have to allow you to be a disappointment to others *to keep you from being puffed up with pride.* Your life is to point others to Jesus and not to you. God has his ways of getting your attention to caution you when you are about to make a wrong decision or you are letting an area of your life get out of the control of the Holy Spirit. It may even be that it is unintentional on your part. But God will allow you to go far enough in the wrong direction so that you will eventually realize that something is not right—you have gotten off course.

Anytime that you get out of God's will, no matter how slight it may be, it usually results in your disappointing somebody. *Despair* is a normal emotion that is felt when you know you have been a disappointment to someone, especially if it was regarding a spiritual concern, and it could have been prevented. When you have failed to respond to God's call upon your life in a certain area, when you have failed to follow through on an opportunity God has provided for you, or when you are just hesitant and slow in a spiritual decision, somebody is going to be disappointed with you. Knowing that you have spiritually disappointed someone is apt to sink you into a time of despair.

We have all experienced making wrong decisions and losing opportunities that will never be available again in quite the same way. The normal response after such mistakes and such lost opportunities is, "if only." There are many "if onlys" we could think of after the fact that would have produced the right results. But then, it is too late, and someone is disappointed in us, and we find ourselves in despair. Such despair is not exceptional. It is very ordinary. It is a natural end of the means produced by no one but ourselves. Although God has allowed it to happen, we cannot blame it on God or anyone else. There are experiences like this in each of our lives when we have just plain blown it. It is unfortunate, but at the same time it can also be fortunate. It is unfortunate in that it could have been prevented, and especially so if you knowingly allowed it to occur. But it is fortunate if it deflates your ego and brings you down to earth again, especially if you have a following of some kind. It shows you that your "fan club" has the potential of dissolving at any time, no matter how successful you may have been.

At the time when Paul wrote 2 Timothy, there were those who were disappointed in Paul. Their spiritual hero was a prisoner. What kind of witness could he have for Christ in prison? Why did he put himself in a position where he got arrested? He may have been able to avoid it if he was smarter. If Paul's God was so great, how come he had not freed Paul from jail? Those were just a few of the questions and comments that were made about Paul's situation from those who had looked to him for spiritual guidance. Yet he was right in the center of God's will for his life.

God used this situation to keep Paul humble, but strong in the Lord. Even to Paul, it seemed as though "all forsook me." That is verse sixteen. But then comes verse seventeen: "But the Lord stood with me and strengthened me, so that the message might be preached fully through me" (2 Tim. 4:17). *But the Lord.* Three wonderful, victorious words! Three life-changing, situation-improving, doubt-erasing, and despair-removing words. The God who disciplines us is also the God who delivers us, even when we have blown it, or as was the case with Paul, it may appear to some that we have failed.

Paul was not a failure. He was right where God wanted him to be. Paul did seem to be disappointed by some of his circumstances, but he allowed it to divinely exercise him so that he had no confidence in anybody or anything but the Lord. Of course, that was the story of Paul's life. He knew, though, that he had much that he could be "puffed up" about (2 Cor. 11:16-12:6; Phil. 3:4-7). So the Lord used disappointing times in Paul's life to keep him from being puffed up with pride and to keep Christ preeminent in his life. Years before his letter to Timothy, Paul wrote these words to the Christians at Rome: "And we know that all things work together for good to those who love God, to those who are the called according to His purpose" (Rom. 8:28). Yes, those words to Paul were more than what has just become in our day a much quoted verse to many Christians. They are really true, if you allow God's divine discipline to exercise you. Paul knew firsthand what he wrote because he knew it from personal experience.

> *The God who disciplines us is also the God who delivers us, even when we have blown it, or as was the case with Paul, it may appear to some that we have failed.*

There is a *dilemma of despair* that comes when you have been a disappointment to others. But there is also a *delight of despair*. The delight of despair comes when you realize what a failure you are in the flesh. The delight is found when you fall down before God, emptied of self-pride, repentant in your heart, totally at his mercy. It is there you find that "underneath are the everlasting arms" (Deut. 33:27). There, you find, instead of receiving God's hand of correction and rebuke, you feel his comfort and reassurance. There, you receive his strength and support that enables you to stand for him, even when you feel that all others have forsaken you.

THAT YOU MAY POINT OTHERS TO CHRIST

If others have told you that you have been a disappointment to them regarding some spiritual matter, then apologize, ask their forgiveness, ask God's forgiveness, and admit your need of his help to live a life that points others to Jesus and not to you. A third reason for divine disappointment is *that you may point others to Christ.* When Christ is preeminent in your life, then your attention is not centered on the wrong person(s) or things. When you are not puffed up with pride, then it takes attention off of you. That makes it possible for you to point others to Christ.

One of the first steps to develop in learning how to point others to Christ is to have a forgiving spirit. You not only need to learn how to forgive others who have wronged you or disappointed you, but you need to seek forgiveness of those you have wronged, offended, or disappointed by something you have done or not done. You may feel that the person you have wronged or offended has done the same to you. But do not let pride get in the way of doing what you ought to do. If you harbor a grudge or animosity toward someone in your heart, you are not living a life that points others to Christ. When you have so much pride that you will not apologize to someone or admit it when you have made a mistake, then you are not living a life that points others to Christ.

At one of the churches where I served as minister of youth, I sensed that something was not right between two girls in our youth group and me. I mentioned this to one of their mothers who had a sweet, cooperative spirit. She acknowledged that her daughter and the other girl did not like the way I did things, and they felt that I did not like them. So I arranged with that mother to come over to her home to meet with her daughter and the other girl.

Some of the best advice I ever received came from another minister in the same town whose daughter was best friends with those two girls. He knew of the problem the two girls had with me because they had talked to him about it. This pastor friend advised me to go into the meeting with the girls solely seeking what I could do on my part to work things out. He felt that if I went in to the meeting and pointed out faults that the girls had, then they would probably be further resentful. Most likely, they would drop out as active members of our youth group.

I followed his advice. When I met with them one Sunday afternoon, I told them that I wanted our relationship to be a good one, so I asked them if they would take a few minutes to share with me what I had done to cause a problem. An hour later they finally got through with me. It was the most humbling and humiliating hour of my life. Most of their judgments about me were not really true. They were basically from misunderstanding all the facts or a lack of good communication. But some of the things they pointed out about me were painfully true. I apologized, I asked their forgiveness, I told them I would change where I needed to do so, and that I wanted to be friends with them. I could have pointed out some things that I thought were wrong with them, but I refrained. We cried some, because they had not really wanted the confrontation. I asked God to forgive me, and I asked for his help to use this experience to be a better minister and a better witness for Christ.

That uncomfortable situation was a freeing experience for me. I had thought that I was a pretty cool youth minister, who really knew how to relate to young people. But I was puffed up with pride. I did, though, allow that incident to exercise me spiritually and ministerially. I can go back to that Sunday afternoon as the place where God purged some things out of my life—things that really were not bad, but things that were keeping me from pointing others to Christ the way he wanted me to do it. I learned a great lesson from "being humbled" by two teenage girls whom God used to point out some "blind spots" in my life that hindered me in my ministry for the Lord.

Although it does not seem to happen too often, the person who said that you were a disappointment to them needs to ask your forgiveness and God's forgiveness too. Christians need to see why this needs to be done. When someone gets down on you and upset because you disappointed them, it actually says of them that they have molded you into their image of what they think you ought to be. When a person gets so disappointed with you that it causes them to be bitter, resentful, and mad, it is an indication of their own spiritual weakness. Those who walk in the Spirit and are trained by God's divine discipline do not become cynical of others who disappoint them, they do not become critical, and they do not have stinging, bitter things to say about those who disappoint them.

Every Christian needs to learn to make room for God to deal directly and personally with other people. That is a commandment God has given to us (Rom. 12:19), but it is one that goes unheeded too many times. If someone has disappointed you, take it to God in the prayer closet and leave it to him to deal with that person. If they are at fault, then he will. But don't play God and try to address that which is in God's hands. Ask God to work through the situation to show you how you can be an encouragement to the one who had disappointed you. It may be that the only thing you can do is pray for them, but that is the first thing you ought to do anyway.

> *It may be that the only thing you can do is pray for them, but that is the first thing you ought to do anyway.*

Paul stated of those who had disappointed him, "May it not be charged against them" (2 Tim. 4:16). That was Paul's prayer to God on behalf of those who had disappointed him. He forgave them, and he interceded on their behalf. Pray and forgive. Pray that the person who has disappointed you will live a life that "looks unto Jesus" (Heb. 12:3), and that they are Spirit filled and Spirit led. A Christian will always pray God's redemption over God's vengeance, although God's vengeance is sometimes the only way God gets a person to the point of redemption.

When you have forgiven those who have disappointed you and you pray for them, and when you have sought forgiveness from those whom you have disappointed, then you can be assured that the Lord will stand with you and strengthen you so that his message might be fully proclaimed through you (2 Tim. 4:17). Your life will point others to Christ. You can also be assured that the Lord will protect you and provide for you (2 Tim. 4:18) as you allow Christ to speak through you and live through you so that others may hear the gospel of Christ.

CONCLUSION

Divine disappointment is for the purpose of getting our affections and focus off anyone or anything that is preeminent above Christ in our lives. It is also to keep us from getting puffed up with pride. Especially for those in positions of spiritual leadership, divine disappointment comes to keep you from developing a "messiah complex" over others and from others so that you will not get spiritually puffed up with pride.

Divine disappointment should draw us to the prayer closet and to our knees. It should get us into the Word and keep us influenced by the Word and not by the world. It shows us how forgiving we are to others who have hurt us and wronged us. It is to make us realize that the great debt of love we owe the Lord for the forgiveness of our sins and his free gift of eternal life in heaven is far greater than the disappointment that others may cause us. It teaches us how to admit our mistakes and ask forgiveness from others. The whole process weeds out hindrances from our lives that keep us from pointing others to Christ as well as we could.

The way you handle divine disappointment is comparable to the level you have reached in your journey of faith. It shows you your spiritual depth as a Christian. May the disappointments that you have caused for others or the disappointments that others have caused you to have not cause you to personally see yourself as a disappointment. If they do, it is because your affections, desires, and focus are on something or someone other than Jesus at this point in your life. It is because you are dwelling on your disappointments. Oh, dear friend, look unto Jesus! Keep Christ preeminent in your life. Let your disappointments work for your good and for his glory. Resolve to make a difference for Jesus that will have eternal benefits for those whom your life reaches for Christ.

10: DIVINE DISTURBANCE

"AT EASE IN ZION"

Divine Disturbance: An experience God may bring upon a church or upon individual Christians in which he breaks up the settled order of our lives to shake us up and wake us up spiritually or to take us spiritually in a new direction.

There is a book whose subject deals with the last words of famous people. We tend to place great importance on the last words people speak before they die. The last words people speak normally address what they feel would be of the greatest benefit to the hearers. What if you knew that you only had a few days or just a few hours left on this earth? What if you knew that you were never going to see someone again? What would you say? Most likely, you would tell them what you felt was the most important thing they could know and do to live life to its fullest and help others to live in such a way. Such a situation is recorded in the Bible in Acts 20:17-37. Those verses reveal that Paul had called the elders of the church at Ephesus to meet him at Miletus, where he saw them for the last time (Acts 20:25). The last words Paul shared gave evidence of his faithful service for the Lord, but they also were words of caution, challenge, comfort, encouragement, and exhortation to the elders addressing what they must do to minister to their "flock" and mature them in the faith.

The Bible records some of the last words Jesus said after his Resurrection and prior to his Ascension. One of the last earthly sayings of our Lord has been given a title. The words of Jesus recorded in Matthew 28:19-20 are known as, "The Great Commission." Those last words, which the Savior spoke to his followers before he ascended into heaven, are just as applicable for us today. We should continue to respect and observe those words as being of the greatest importance. This chapter will center upon those last words which Jesus spoke on this earth and upon one of the divine disciplines God uses to see that we heed those last words.

Just before he was "taken up" (Acts 1:9), Jesus told his followers, "But you shall receive power when the Holy Spirit has come upon you; and you shall be witnesses to Me in Jerusalem, and in all Judea and Samaria, and to the end of the earth" (Acts 1:8). The Lord's words to that small group of believers, who originally heard those words, was to establish the church in Jerusalem, then to branch out into the neighboring regions, even into the land of those they despised—the Samaritans. But they were not to stop their witness for Christ in their corner of the world. They were to take the gospel throughout the world. Because of their faithfulness to fulfill the last words that Christ spoke to them, we have the blessed privilege and opportunity of responding to the gospel and receiving the gift of eternal life in heaven.

At times, though, God has had to use the divine discipline of *divine disturbance* to keep the church awake, alive, pure, and on the move, penetrating the world with the gospel of Christ. Otherwise, the good news of Jesus may not have come to our end of the earth. After the church at Jerusalem had established a witness for Christ there, God allowed a divine disturbance to come upon the believers to move them on into the world to proclaim salvation through Christ Jesus.

The Bible says that following the stoning of Stephen, "a great persecution arose against the church which was at Jerusalem; and they were all scattered throughout the regions of Judea and Samaria" (Acts 8:1). *Acts 8:1 was necessary for Acts 1:8 to be fulfilled.* The church at Jerusalem was growing daily (Acts 2:47). They had a warm, loving spirit

150

and atmosphere in their new found family of faith. They were all in one accord (Acts 2:44; 4:32). They liked being where they were and what they had in their church family at Jerusalem. But Jesus had told them that they were to be his witnesses beyond Jerusalem. So God allowed a divine disturbance to scatter the church in order to gather new believers and establish new churches in those places to which they fled. The Bible records that "those who were scattered went everywhere preaching the word" (Acts 8:35) by proclaiming Christ (Acts 8:4, 35). The purpose of this divine disturbance was to take the church spiritually and physically beyond Jerusalem.

By the time one gets to chapter eight of Acts, two other purposes for divine disturbance have been revealed. In Acts 2, a purpose of the divine disturbance which occurred on the Day of Pentecost was to wake up the church spiritually to fulfill the mission to which God had called her: to evangelize the world by the empowering of the Holy Spirit.

The purpose of the divine disturbances the believers experienced in Acts 4, when they were arrested and threatened, and the incident with Ananias and Sapphira in Acts 5, were disturbances that came to shake the church up spiritually, physically, mentally, and emotionally in directing and confirming the central focus of their lives on the fulfillment of God's will. Those disturbances centered their spiritual focus in drawing the believers closer together in their emotional bonds as they prayed for holy boldness to physically withstand whatever and whoever tried to hinder and halt their witness for Christ. The incident with Ananias and Sapphira brought a healthy fear upon the people toward the greatness and holiness of God. It showed them the necessity for the church to be morally pure and mentally alert to the kinds of influences that would hurt the church spiritually.

A disturbance is a break-up of the settled order. It causes us to be inconvenienced. It can also lead to emotional, mental, physical, and spiritual upset. The book of Acts reveals three reasons for divine disturbance: to shake us up spiritually; to wake us up spiritually; and to take us spiritually in a new direction. This chapter will examine why God not only allows but he may even break up the settled order of our lives through divine disturbance.

To Shake Us Up Spiritually

The late Vance Havner has been quoted as saying, "Most Christians sacrifice to the point of inconvenience." How true that is today of too many Christians who talk commitment and dedication for the Lord as long as things are comfortable. But if the Christian life begins to call for service that is inconvenient or discomfiting, then the commitment and dedication in their talk of faith are not lived out in their walk of faith. Commitment and dedication to Christ and his church are more than two hours on Sunday mornings, another hour or two on Sunday evenings, and an hour or two on Wednesday nights. It is even more than the faithful few who come out for church visitation one night a week. It is even more than a several night commitment and follow-through to attend revival services two or three times a year, or making a similar commitment to work in Vacation Bible School or some other special emphasis of your church. You can be doing all those things and still not be dedicated to the central focus of your life being the fulfillment of God's will. Commitment and dedication to Christ and his church are to be year long and life long.

> *God may send divine disturbance into your life to shake you up spiritually so that you rededicate yourself to doing his will.*

You can be doing many good things in the Christian life and still not be doing the right things. There is something that is more important than knowing the will of God and being in the will of God. You need to *do* the will of God. Even when you may know God's will for your life, and you are in his will in that you are in the right place and position to fulfill it, you may not be doing it as God wants you to do it. In this case, God may send divine disturbance into your life *to shake you up spiritually* so that you rededicate yourself to doing his will. You can even be doing a beehive of activity in your church, but you may discover you are doing a little bit of everything and getting a whole lot of nothing done, when you step back and evaluate what all your activity is accomplishing for the cause of Christ. So where priorities have gotten out of order, the result is disturbance. Sometimes, God sends the disturbance, but often we have no one to blame but ourselves. God's purpose either way is to shake us up emotionally and mentally so that spiritually we rededicate the central focus of our lives on the fulfillment of his intended will in that area of our lives.

After I had been in the youth ministry for a few years, there was a period when I became divinely disturbed. I knew that God had called me to serve him at that time as a youth minister. I knew that he wanted me at the church where I was on the staff. Although the outward signs pointed to a successful youth program, I did not feel successful. I was disturbed and unsettled in my spirit. I did not have any hidden or unconfessed sins in my life that were causing the disturbance. We could attract large crowds for youth events and saw many decisions whenever an altar call was given. We had a full schedule of activities and a sizeable budget to cover costs. But I was not seeing the outward evidence that Jesus was really making a difference daily in the lives of those young people.

God divinely disturbed me to get me to see that having a lot of unique, fun activities which attracted big numbers of youth was not bad, but what kind of significant, life-changing spiritual differences was my great-looking program on paper making in real life? The Lord divinely disturbed me so that I would rededicate my life and my ministry to those things that would make the greatest impact for Christ. He used divine disturbance to show me that the central focus of fulfilling his will for my life as a minister of youth was in teaching teenagers how to deny themselves from the pull of the world by taking up their crosses daily and following Jesus. That was the way those teenagers would best impact their world for Christ.

As I rededicated myself to that purpose, the numbers of young people who responded to such an emphasis did not bring phenomenal growth in numbers, but the impact for Christ was greater as those committed youth began making a difference for Jesus. They are still making a difference today in the churches where they serve as ministers or as committed lay people. More people were reached for Christ by those more spiritually committed youth, who learned how to be different in order to make a difference for Jesus, than by the large numbers of youth who were attracted to events where their lives and the lives of those around them were not significantly changed.

That is the story of how the Lord used divine disturbance to shake me up spiritually. I was not purposely trying to do something contrary to his will. But he wanted me to do it a different way, which was the best way. The best way, God's way, always makes a greater difference for Jesus. If God is shaking you up spiritually, the divine disturbance is to get you to reevaluate what you are in comparison to what you should be at this point in your life concerning God's will. The result should be for you to remove from your life what is inhibiting the fulfillment of his will. Then there should be the *rededication* of your life to the Lord so that in all things and at all times you will be a witness for Christ, God's way.

TO WAKE US UP SPIRITUALLY

A second reason why God allows divine disturbance to come upon our lives is *to wake us up spiritually*. On the Day of Pentecost, the church was awakened spiritually because the Holy Spirit came in power upon the church. The Holy Spirit empowered the church to fulfill her purpose and mission of evangelizing the world (see Matt. 28:19-20; Acts 1:8). The process began there, but it did not end there. The book of Acts is a stirring testimony for the early church of their faithfulness to do their part in fulfilling the Great Commission. It is a mission, though, that is still incomplete. Those last words of Christ are as relevant for the church today as they were for the first church.

When the word *evangelism* is used in this book, I have in mind a definition used by Dr. B. Gray Allison, president emeritus of Mid-America Baptist Theological Seminary, in the personal evangelism classes he taught: "To so present Jesus Christ to men that under the conviction, inspiration, and leadership of the Holy Spirit, they may see their need of the Savior, accept Jesus Christ as Lord and Savior, and serve Him through one of His churches." I also have in mind with the word *evangelism* that one is not truly evangelized until the convert is actively involved in a local church. The process of evangelism involves the evangelized becoming evangelizers. That is the basic mission of the church. Much more is involved in the function of a church, but without the basic priority of evangelism eventually there would not be a church.

A phrase from Amos 6:1 is sometimes applicable to churches today: "Woe to you who are at ease in Zion." Many of our churches today have everything that a country club has, in the way of facilities and recreation, other than a golf course (I don't know of any church that has its own golf course!). You could spend all your time isolated within your church "campus," attending worship services, committee meetings, and Bible studies. It is even possible that while your children are in class at your church's Christian school, you can get a physical workout at your church's recreation center and sports complex. With the massive church facilities around today, there is no shortage of options to choose from where you could spend your spare time *"at ease in Zion."*

> "We need to get outside the stained-glass windows, out there in the highways and byways, where they crucify Messiahs."

Please understand that those who are so totally involved in the amenities of their church campus are not doing bad things. At such churches, you can be involved in some of those amenities, where you are able to do so without the negative influences of the sinful world. But you may stay too isolated and insulated from the world inside your church world. As a result, you are not negatively influenced by the world, but you are not positively influencing the world for Christ. We are to be separate from the world in our conduct and conversation, but we are not to be isolated from the world. We are to be witnesses for Jesus in this world. I once heard a preacher say, "We need to get outside the stained-glass windows, out there in the highways and byways, where they crucify Messiahs." Our local church is to be the primary source of our spiritual involvement where we are educated and motivated to go out and influence our world for Christ. Our church is not to be a place where we spend all our time isolated from those who need to be reached for Christ.

Big, beautiful church buildings are actually spiritually worthless, multi-million dollar properties if people who are unsaved and unchurched drive by them and never see the people of those churches alive for Christ, out in the world beyond the church walls, making a difference for Jesus.

I am not saying that every church with such facilities is growing into themselves. I had the privilege of serving on the staff of a church whose facilities were second to none. Over three years, we saw hundreds of people get saved. We saw many lives bettered and broken lives mended. The major reason, though, that most of the super churches with varied, expansive facilities and programs are having astounding numerical growth is because of transfer growth—Christians coming from other churches who do not have all the nice facilities and multifaceted programs. The danger of it is that such a church can basically become an exclusive Christian club that caters to keeping its members entertained and happy, instead of being a hospital for sinners and a first aid station for battered, broken, bruised, and wounded saints.

When a church begins enjoying its luxuries and getting too comfortable in the sanctuary and security of their church grounds, it is a prime candidate for a divine disturbance. Great wealth and comfortable lifestyles may make people think that they are secure and blessed of God. But a big Baptist country club (it does not matter what denomination it is—I used mine) does not glorify God and win others to Christ any more than the most prestigious country club in your city.

God sends divine disturbance to churches that are spiritually comatose. They are churches that are going through all the motions of being a church, yet their members do not love Jesus as much as they did when they first met him. These churches are like the church at Ephesus (Rev. 2:1-7), "the church that had everything but the one thing it needed the most." The Lord had complimentary things to say about the church at Ephesus. It was a busy church and had made some great accomplishments. But the Lord warned its members that their church was on the verge of spiritual extinction because they had left their first love. The Lord's word to the church at Ephesus was that *you don't love me like you did when you first met me*. It was a case of faded love. As a result, first things were not first anymore. The members of the church had misplaced priorities. That was all that was wrong with them, but to the Lord that was everything. When your love for Jesus fades, the effect of all the accomplishments and all the busy work fades and proves ineffective and insincere.

God wants a church that is *evangelistically awake and alive* for Him. A church that is awake and alive for Christ is made up of Christians who are awake and alive for Christ. The church is God's people. The mission of the church is to live, show, and share Jesus. As Christians are called to be separate from the world in our lifestyle, we are also called to go into the world with the message of Jesus Christ. When people, especially the unchurched and the unsaved, look at a church building, they should not see it as a monument to God in the manner we look at the monuments erected to our conquests and heroes. Rather, they should see the church as a living church, as people who are visible around them, reaching out, sharing Jesus, and bringing the unchurched and the unsaved into the worship, education, and fellowship of the church.

> *God wants a church that is evangelistically awake and alive for Him.*

When God sends divine disturbance to wake us up spiritually, its intended purpose is to bring *revival.* It is to get our spiritual lives centered upon our witness for Christ in penetrating the world around us with the gospel. *Revival is the church getting spiritually right with God and one another.* It occurs when each of us gets our eyes off what someone else needs to do and each of us looks personally inside ourselves to see what "I" need to change to be right with God and with my fellow brother or sister in Christ. The result of the church getting spiritually right is that people get saved. The unchurched and the unsaved begin to see a church that is awake and alive, reaching out beyond their walls in the name of Jesus, proclaiming the good news of Jesus, and adding converts to the family of faith which congregates at their local church.

During divine disturbance, self-examine and corporately examine yourselves in the light of God's Word to see what changes God wants you to make in your personal lives and in your church. Then, as revival comes, get ready to see great and mighty things happen that you have never seen happen before through the ministry of your church as it impacts the world around you for Christ.

TO TAKE US SPIRITUALLY IN A NEW DIRECTION

God divinely disturbed the believers at Jerusalem by allowing persecution to come upon them in order to take them spiritually in a new direction, providing a third reason for which God divinely disturbs us: *to take us spiritually in a new direction*. For the church at Jerusalem, divine disturbance came about to move them beyond the fellowship and discipleship of their home church in order to evangelize and establish new churches throughout the world. That is what Jesus had told them they were to do.

Those early days of the church at Jerusalem had to be exciting times. People were being saved and added to the church every day. There was such a sweet spirit in that church. They had all things in common and shared everything they had materially with one another. No one felt out of place and uncomfortable when they came to worship at the church at Jerusalem. It was a joyful, exhilarating church. If God had not allowed persecution to come upon the church, it would have taken much longer before the gospel would have been taken to the regions of Judea and Samaria, and to the end of the earth. Something had to be done to get those Christians beyond the comfort and security of their fellowship because their new found faith in Christ was not to be exclusive only to those who came to Jerusalem. So God allowed that comfort and security to be removed, and it moved the church on into the world.

God may have to bring divine disturbance into your life, at times, to take you spiritually in a new direction. Divine disturbance can come into your life even when you are faithfully and obediently serving the Lord where you are right now. It is for the purpose of *redirection*. God may simply desire for you *to serve him somewhere else or some other way*.

The reason God sends divine disturbance into your life may be to take you somewhere else to serve him where the need is greater for the special abilities God has given you. When divine disturbance comes into your life, and you know that you are in God's will, then the Lord is wanting to redirect you spiritually. He may move you or he may keep you where you are. He may want you to begin a newer or different emphasis or area of ministry where you are. His will may take you somewhere else to do what you are presently doing or it may be to go somewhere else to do something completely different from what you are doing in your service for him now. By the way, you do not have to be a professional minister for the Lord to direct and redirect your life in such a manner. When you are facing career moves in a secular job, God has a spiritual purpose for moving you, if that is how he leads you. Your accepting a job in another city can and should work two ways. When you find a new church home, you and your family may be the ones who are needed to fill positions of leadership in your new church. You are an answer to prayer for a need in that church. Your acceptance of a new job not only is of personal benefit to you, but it is of spiritual benefit to the church you join upon your moving to a new location. If God is divinely disturbing you, just be sensitive to the fact that God may want to move you beyond what you are presently doing for him and where you are presently serving him.

If God sends divine disturbance for the purpose of taking you spiritually in a new direction, his intent is to redirect you to serve him somewhere else or some other way. There are signs that will show you how God wants the divine disturbance to redirect you. The place to begin is to seek his guidance through the Bible and in prayer. He will give you direction and confirm it through the scriptures, the Holy Spirit, through the counsel of godly saints, and by opportunities opening up for you to consider. Be assured God's guidance will never be contrary to the scriptures, the Holy Spirit will never prompt you to disobey the Word of God, the advice of other Christians will not lead you to do something unscriptural, and the available opportunities for consideration will not cause you to compromise spiritually. You then need to follow the route which opens up through the providence of God, which is affirmed as the direction in which you are to go by the peace in your heart and the fruitful results of your witness and work for the Lord.

Determining Specifically the Purpose of Divine Disturbance

You may be wondering, now that you have learned the reasons why God brings divine disturbance into your life, "How do I know for certain which one applies to my situation?" In determining how God specifically wants to use divine disturbance in your life, it can be simplified into two basic steps: prayer and providence.

Always make prayer your first choice, not your last resort, as often seems to be the case for us, when trying to find the will of God concerning a matter. As you spend time in communion with God, he will show you his will. For example, while Peter was praying one day (Acts 10:9-43), the Lord clearly revealed that he had a new direction for Peter's ministry. Peter was to take the gospel to the Gentiles. It was new territory to venture into at the time. The Jews had few dealings with the Gentiles in those days, so this new area of ministry for Peter could possibly be met with opposition and misunderstanding by his fellow Jews. But as he was praying, God clearly confirmed his will to Peter three times (Acts 10:16). It was confirmed again as he finished praying (Acts 10:17-20). A Gentile named Cornelius had also been praying. He was seeking to really get to know God. The Lord confirmed that his prayers had been answered (Acts 10:4). Cornelius was told to go and get Peter.

God divinely disturbed two godly men while they were praying. He used an angel to disturb Cornelius and a vision to disturb Peter. The divine providence of God was working in all this too. It was affirmed as Peter went to the home of Cornelius. There he preached Jesus (Acts 10:36), and the Gentiles who heard him believed unto salvation. The process was put into motion with prayer. Peter prayed and sensed God's guidance, which the Lord confirmed. As God was working providentially in several different ways, Peter followed the promptings of the Lord. At first, he was not exactly sure what the divine disturbance from God was for, but he went where God led him. It was providentially affirmed through the belief unto salvation of those to whom God had sent Peter.

Another similar experience happened to Paul. There was a time when Paul wanted to take the gospel to Asia. But God divinely disturbed Paul as the Holy Spirit prompted him not to preach there (Acts 16:6-7). Through a vision, God divinely disturbed Paul that he was to take the gospel to Macedonia (Acts 16:9-10). Paul then went there as the first missionary to preach the gospel in Europe. God providentially led Paul and his companions away from where they had thought they ought to go. The Lord confirmed it, and then he affirmed it through people being won to Christ from the moment that Paul and his missionary partners entered Macedonia.

Therefore, make prayer an integral, active part of your daily life. As the Lord brings divine disturbance into your life and as you spend time with him in prayer, you will sense his direction. As seen in the examples from the lives of Peter and Paul, a divine disturbance could occur undeniably while you are praying. But regardless of when the divine disturbance occurs, keep praying until you get a sense of his direction. God will confirm it in a way that you understand it.

Always start with the scriptures. Ask God to give you a confirmation from his Word, if his direction is not clear cut. If he does not give you a specific verse, then make sure that the way you are feeling led is not contrary to the Bible. As previously emphasized, you can be assured that God will never lead you to do something which contradicts a truth or principle of the Bible. God also confirms what he says to you in prayer through other means, such as the promptings of the Holy Spirit, the counsel of godly Christians, and an overwhelming sense of peace in your heart. His guidance through those means, too, will never direct you to do anything which is contrary to the scriptures.

> *Regardless of when the divine disturbance occurs, keep praying until you get a sense of his direction.*

The providence of God will show you the purpose of divine disturbance and if you are being redirected as God desires. He affirms it as you see souls saved and lives bettered through the influence of your life. When you are not absolutely sure if you are to go somewhere else and where you are to go, it is best to stay put until God clearly reveals to you when and where you are to go. But remain actively involved in the work of the Lord where you are and keep doing the things a Christian ought to be doing.

Conclusion

Someone has said that if the church is not in the middle of a storm, she is just coming out of one or about to enter one. God has planned it that way. It is to keep the church spiritually on her toes and on the move. Otherwise, if the church is "at ease in Zion," she may neglect the world beyond her walls. When it is needed, God sends or allows divine disturbance to break up our settled order. He may need to *shake us up* spiritually so that we will reevaluate our lives and remove what is hindering us in the fulfillment of his perfect will for our lives. Thus, there is the rededication of our life to the Lord in all our ways. Rededicated Christians are more focused spiritually on the things that matter the most. The church is only as strong as the spiritual commitment and maturity of her members and a positive result of divine disturbance is stronger, properly focused churches.

The Lord may also use divine disturbance to *wake us up* spiritually. It is to get a church out of a spiritual rut in which the members are going through the motions of what a church ought to be, but the spiritual fervor is not there. The intended purpose of this kind of divine disturbance is to bring revival. A spiritually revived church has a profound effect and influence upon the world around it by making an eternal difference in the lives of those the church is able to touch and reach for Christ.

A third purpose of divine disturbance is to take you spiritually to serve the Lord somewhere else or some other way. He causes disturbance to redirect your life.

The means of disturbance has not been emphasized in this chapter. But from the experiences of the Bible personalities who have been used as examples, we have seen that the Lord used persecution, visions, angels, promptings of the Holy Spirit, life situations, and the influence of other people as his means for disturbance. There are other ways by which God disturbs us. It always involves a break up of the settled order of what you have been accustomed to. I have experienced divine disturbance through something as intangible as a restlessness in my spirit. There were no outward, visible, tangible signs to give evidence that God was disturbing my life. When God sends divine disturbance upon your life, the outward evidence can be all around you or it may not be so clear to see. You will know it, though, and so will some others around you, even some who are not part of your church life or spiritual environment. The important thing is that you need to let divine disturbance exercise you for its intended purpose. It will then have a positive effect on your life and on the lives of others.

Divine disturbance has been covered in this chapter from the perspective of Christians who are sincere in their walk of faith and who are striving to be obedient to God. They may not be totally within his will, but they are not purposely disobeying God. But divine disturbance can come into a person's life when he or she is disobediently running from or resisting the will of God. God sent divine disturbance upon Jonah in the literal form of a storm (Jonah 1:4, 12) and in the literal form of a great fish that swallowed him (Jonah 1:17). He was as good as dead for the three days he spent in the belly of that big fish. But he got right with God, and the Lord used him to bring about one of the greatest revivals ever (see Jonah 3).

If you feel that you are in the midst of divine disturbance, whatever the reason may be that God has brought it upon you, it is for your good and for the good of others. As God uses it to make you a more effective witness for him, others will be won to Christ through your life and their lives will be eternally changed for the best. Other Christians will be affected positively, whether it is those who are experiencing divine disturbance with you in a church or those who will be impacted from divine disturbance's intended effect on you. You will have the joy of being used to bring glory and honor to God. Through the intended purpose of divine disturbance, your life will ultimately count for Christ and for that which is of eternal value.

11: Divine Drudgery

"Living Out the Glory of God"

Divine Drudgery: The daily routine of life of doing the same things over and over again, which is the norm for most Christians, but it is the basic means by which God has chosen to manifest his manifold grace to the world.

Then He went down with them and came to Nazareth, and was subject to them, but His mother kept all these things in her heart. And Jesus increased in wisdom and stature, and in favor with God and men. (Luke 2:51-52)

One of the greatest hindrances of the Christian life is that we think we have to do big things for the Lord. Success in the world, and unfortunately, even in many Christian circles, is based on doing something big and great. What big things did Jesus do during those eighteen years of silence about his life from age twelve, when he astonished the synagogue teachers with his understanding and answers (Luke 2:46-47), to the beginning of his public ministry at about age thirty (Luke 3:23). His daily routine or lifestyle during those "silent years" was what many in our society today would look upon as drudgery. He worked in his earthly father's carpenter shop. He memorized the Law, the Prophets, and the Writing. He studied. He prayed. He helped out in the chores at home. He was subject (obedient) to his parents. He developed godly character. He increased in wisdom and stature and in favor with God and men.

How did Moses become a man of godly character, able to lead the Israelites out of Egyptian bondage? God took him from the luxuries and comforts of royalty, as the adopted son of Pharaoh's daughter, to feeding sheep for forty years in the desert. But this developed such character in him, that even though God did do big things through Moses, he was referred to by God as the most humble man on the face of the earth (Num. 12:3). He was not a perfect man, and he knew what it was to be punished by God. But the Bible says that the Lord God spoke to Moses face to face, as a man speaks to his friend (Exod. 33:11). That came about because Moses was conformed to the character and will of God. That was what forty years of divine delay (chapter six) did for Moses, but it was also forty years in which Moses also experienced the divine discipline of *divine drudgery*.

A final divine discipline which this book will address is that of divine drudgery. Drudgery is a work, routine, or way of life which is usually hard, tedious, tiresome, and most often, menial. It is the norm for the Christian life. Most Christians will not be known on this earth for the big and great things they have done. Drudgery is repulsive to the standards the world has set for enjoyment, happiness, satisfaction, and success. But drudgery is not repulsive to God. It is the basic means by which he has chosen to manifest himself to the world. If we will learn to accept it in its positive sense, divine drudgery is where we develop the kind of character that bears a family resemblance to Jesus. It is where we see the manifold grace of God manifested on a daily basis within our lives. It is where we see the deity of Jesus Christ exhibited the greatest on this earth, as we find that it is in divine drudgery where we are of our greatest worth to God. Through divine drudgery, the supernatural works of God blend into the providence of God, working mostly within the natural laws of mankind, nature, and the atmosphere in which we live. It is where the glory of God we have seen and experienced on the mountaintop is lived out among the people in the valleys of life where we live.

> *Divine drudgery is the divine discipline that more Christians will need to learn to endure so that they may be divinely exercised by it.*

Divine drudgery is the divine discipline that more Christians will need to learn to endure so that they may be divinely exercised by it. In a world whose mindset tends to look at doing the same thing over and over again, year after year, as being uninteresting, unexciting, and showing a lack of initiative, it is what God calls the vast majority of Christians to do in life. But in the steadiness and consistency of drudgery, the *greatness of God*, the *grace of God*, and the *glory of God* are most personally, impressively, and influentially manifested in the world today.

REVEALING THE GREATNESS OF GOD

One of the characteristics used numerously in the Bible to describe God is his greatness. Moses described the greatness of God this way:

> *O Lord God, You have begun to show Your servant Your greatness and Your mighty hand, for what god is there in heaven or on earth who can do anything like Your works and Your mighty deeds? (Deut. 3:24).*

David said of God's greatness:

> *Yours, O Lord, is the greatness, the power and the glory, the victory and the majesty; For all that is in heaven and in the earth is Yours; Yours is the kingdom, O Lord, and You are exalted as head over all. Both riches and honor come from You, and You reign over all. In Your hand is power and might; In Your hand it is to make great and to give strength to all. (1 Chron. 29:11-12)*

Those verses give a model representation for the many verses in the Bible that refer to the greatness of God.

The word *greatness* is an accurate term to use in describing God because nothing can exceed the greatness of God. God is great for many different reasons, but Paul revealed the greatness of God which matters the most to us: "And what is the exceeding greatness of His power toward us who believe, according to the working of His mighty power which He worked in Christ when He raised Him from the dead" (Eph. 1:19-20). The greatness of God which matters the most to us is shown through Jesus. God's love for us was so great that he sent his Son that we might be saved (John 3:16-17). He allowed Jesus to die as the penalty for our sins so that we could receive the forgiveness of our sins and the gift of eternal life through faith and belief in Jesus as our Lord and Savior (Rom. 5:8; Eph. 2:8-9; Acts 16:31).

There was no greater love (John 15:13) that could be shown for us by God and by our Lord Jesus than the Cross of Calvary. The classic gospel song, "How Great Thou Art," says it so well:

> *And when I think that God, His Son not sparing,*
> *Sent Him to die, I scarce can take it in;*
> *That on the cross, my burden gladly bearing,*
> *He bled and died to take away my sin;*
> *Then sings my soul, my Savior God to thee;*
> *How great thou art, how great thou art!*
> *Then sings my soul, my Savior God to thee;*
> *How great thou art, how great thou art!*[16]

That is the greatness of God which matters the most to us—our eternal salvation. We see much of the greatness of God around us every day in this world he created. But someday, these earthly things will pass away. God has created a new world, though, which will endure forever (Rev. 21:1; 22:5). We inherit the eternal kingdom of God through placing our faith, belief, and trust in Jesus as our Lord and Savior (1 Pet. 1:3-5). But there are those who will never know the greatness of God which matters the most, unless those of us who do know reveal it to them.

You may be wondering by now, "What does divine drudgery have to do with revealing the greatness of God?" It is the means by which we can most effectively reveal the greatness of God. When Jesus came to earth as the Messiah, he performed miracles as signs to reveal who he was (John 2:11) so that the people would believe in him. But there were also times when the Lord stressed to the people the importance of believing in him without having to see miracles for proof (John 4:48; Matt. 16:1-4). It is interesting that most of those who saw the miracles he performed never put their faith and belief in him as the Messiah.

We still have those today who are looking for miracles. To them, if Christianity is real, then you ought to be doing something big and great for God, with signs and wonders as the proof. But signs and wonders are not the greatest way by which Jesus is revealed to our world today. We have the Word of God, the Bible, which the Lord has given to us

---

16. Stuart K. Hine, *How Great Thou Art*, (Manna Music, 1953, Renewed 1981).

to be our absolute authority and supreme source of direction for life. The church in the first century did not have this whole counsel of God we have today in the Holy Bible. So the Lord spoke to them by more visible means. If you want to see a miracle, then get a Bible and read it. It will change your life, as it is a Living Word that will speak to you as you read it. How the Bible came together in its present form was a miracle. Through the centuries, there have been those who have tried to destroy the Bible and those who believe in what it proclaims. But the miracle of the Word continued on, and it continues today, and it will continue forever (Matt. 24:35; Mark 13:31).

Today we also have the inner witness of the Holy Spirit, who indwells those who have been saved (John 14:16-17; Eph. 1:12-14). Then we have, too, the witness of men and women which has passed down through the centuries, testifying that Jesus is Lord and Savior. Jesus told the doubting Thomas, "Because you have seen Me, you have believed. Blessed are those who have not seen and yet have believed" (John 20:29). Peter later expressed it this way: "Jesus Christ, whom having not seen you love. Though now you do not see Him, yet believing, you rejoice with joy inexpressible and full of glory, receiving the end of your faith—the salvation of your souls" (1 Pet. 1:7-9).

Revealing the greatness of God which matters the most—the salvation of souls through Jesus Christ—does not require you to perform miracles. It does require you to reveal Christ through the conduct and conversation of your life (Phil. 1:27).

Oswald Chambers said, "We look for miracles, for eye opening tangibles, and we never dream that all the time God is in the commonplace things and people around us. One of the most amazing revelations of God comes when we learn that it is in the commonplace things that the deity of Jesus Christ is realized."[17] We develop godly character through divine drudgery which brings out in us a family resemblance to Jesus. That is how Christ is deified in the commonplace things. It is through our being faithful to live for the Lord wherever he may have placed us in life. For most of us, it is doing the same work day after day, year after year, not receiving much recognition for it, and not being known except by those in the little corner of the world where we live. It is doing

---

17. Chambers, *My Utmost for His Highest*, 27.

what the "health, wealth, and success" crowd would call drudgery. But I call it divine drudgery because it is where others can most closely and personally see Jesus and meet Jesus through us.

A little boy was walking along a beach where hundreds of starfish were washing onto the shore as the tide was going out. Knowing that they would die without a way back to the water, the young boy would pick one up and throw it back, and continued doing so as he walked along the beach. A pessimistic, older man was observing the boy, and after a few minutes he went up to the lad and asked, "Do you really think that you are making any difference?" The boy picked up another starfish, threw it back into the ocean, looked at the man, and said, "It made a difference to that one." The boy did not do anything big and great in the eyes of most of the world that day. It did not receive the attention of the news media from all over the world. There was not a multi-million dollar rescue effort to save a few hundred starfish from what was a normal act of nature. The boy did not save hundreds of starfish, but he did save some of them. His life made a difference to those his life was able to touch in his little corner of the world, performing an act that after a few minutes would be drudgery to most people.

> *[Divine drudgery] is where others can most closely and personally see Jesus and meet Jesus through us.*

In a day when we have seen big and great ministries experience big and great falls, as a result of the temptations and trappings of worldly success, it is through divine drudgery where the greatest impact for Christ will be made today. You may not reach hundreds for Christ, but you can make a difference in some lives. If we would all do our part right where we are, that is the most effective method of evangelism to reach the unsaved in a shorter period of time than any other way. Divine drudgery is the way by which most of us will have the opportunity and privilege to reveal the greatness of God as manifested in Jesus. Let us make a difference for Christ today.

Relating the Grace of God

Divine drudgery is not only a means by which we can most effectively reveal the greatness of God, but it is also where we see the manifold grace of God manifested on a daily basis within our lives. We so often think only of the grace of God as his unmerited favor in saving us from the penalty of sins by his provision for salvation through Jesus Christ. But there are other elements of God's marvelous, amazing grace, other than his saving grace. The divine discipline of drudgery is where other elements of the manifold grace of God are manifested in your life. As God's grace is lived out through your life, you become a means of *relating the grace of God* to others.

Why do you need to draw from the grace of God in divine drudgery, maybe even more so than in any of the other divine disciplines? A thought by Oswald Chambers on this subject provides convincing insight:

> *It takes Almighty grace to take the next step when there is no vision and no spectator—the next step in devotion, the next step in your study, in your reading, in your kitchen; the next step in your duty, when there is no vision from God, no enthusiasm and no spectator. It takes far more of the grace of God, far more conscious drawing upon God to take that step, than it does to preach the Gospel.*[18]

Since becoming a pastor in 1991, I have come to understand what Mr. Chambers was saying, particularly in the last statement of that quote. The people of the churches I have pastored have been so kind and gracious. After every sermon I have preached, I have received favorable comments. But I wonder, how many of those in our churches who have served faithfully in a position week after week, year after year, and seldom, if ever, receive any recognition, a thank you, or a favorable comment for their service? I know that there are many who do, and they keep on doing so because the grace of God is on them to perform a task faithfully and cheerfully, whether anyone acknowledges them or not, because they do it heartily as to the Lord (Col. 3:23).

Two dear ladies come to my mind who were members of a church where I served as an associate minister over three decades ago, who

---

18. Ibid., 47.

beautifully illustrate faithfulness in the less noticed positions. I am thinking of a mother and daughter. Their modest home was located on a small side street less than a hundred yards from the front door of their church sanctuary. At the time, the mother was nearing ninety years old. She had taught Sunday school for over seventy years. At sixteen years of age, she began teaching a class of six-year-old girls, until she married at twenty-one years of age. After she gave birth to her second child, she started teaching again and had done it continuously for over sixty years. Most of those years were spent teaching in the youth Sunday school department. When she got into her seventies, she became teacher of the oldest ladies Sunday school class because she felt that she could not keep up with the youth in their activities. In addition to teaching Sunday school, she taught the Sunday school lesson two other times each week to the residents of two nursing homes, a ministry she had fulfilled for years. I never heard her complain once about her church or about anything. Even during some times when physical problems kept her from being able to teach, she maintained a positive outlook toward life and a submissive attitude toward the Lord.

Her daughter, who never married, served as secretary of the youth Sunday school department for many years. You would not find anyone else more faithful and committed to her place of service than she was. She worked in a local factory on an assembly line for many years, until the plant closed out operations in her town. I never heard her complain about her job, her church, or anything else. She was sad when her job phased out, but it was not too long before an opportunity came to keep two infants during the day. She performed that work as if those two infants were her own children.

If I gave the names of those two ladies, it would not ring a mental bell as someone you recognized for nearly all who will read this book. If time and space allowed me to tell you more about those sweet ladies, there would be those who would think this mother and daughter lived a sub-standard lifestyle. Some may even call their routine of life a drudgery. I would categorize their lifestyle as divine drudgery, as this book is defining this subject. In it, they have related the grace of God in such a glorious way. If I mentioned the name of a son and brother of those two ladies, many who read this book would know of him. He was a well-known pastor and leader in the Southern Baptist Convention, especially in the 1980s. But he would agree with me that his accomplishments in the ministry were no more significant or any greater in God's eyes than the less noticed and less recognized service of his mother and sister.

Oswald Chambers made another thought provoking observation concerning divine drudgery when he said,

> *We do not need the grace of God to stand crises, human nature and pride are sufficient, we can face the strain magnificently; but it does require the supernatural grace of God to live twenty-four hours in every day as a saint, to go through drudgery as a disciple, to live an ordinary, unobserved ignored existence as a disciple of Jesus. It is inbred in us that we have to do exceptional things for God; but we have not. We have to be exceptional in the ordinary things, to be holy in mean streets, among mean people, and this is not learned in five minutes.*[19]

Why is supernatural grace required? Because to live such a life—a life of drudgery in the world's eyes—goes against the status quo, against our human nature. No, it is not learned in a few minutes or in the best intensive Christian life seminar you could attend for several hours every day for a week. It is learned day after day, week after week, month after month, year after year, through the manifestation of God's grace in the divine discipline of drudgery. In my life, I have found that it is not divine darkness, divine delay, divine differences, divine difficulty, divine disappointment, or divine disturbance where I have felt the most like God has taken his blessings somewhere else. It is in divine drudgery! It is when those periods of time have come in the ministry when it is the same routine week by week with nothing big and great seemingly being accomplished through my life and ministry. Somewhere else things appear to be happening big spiritually, and it seems like everybody knows about it. And, oh, I want to see it happen where I am!

God, though, has not called us all to be just alike and to do everything the same way. He has called us to be faithful. Some are to do more planting, some are to do more watering, but God will provide the increase (1 Cor. 3:6-7). If you keep faithfully at it year after year, you

---

19. Ibid., 218.

may never see the big and great things happen, but you will be able to look back and see that God gave the increase in his way and in his time, steadily, the way that has lasting results. If you and I will be faithful to serve the Lord, not just because duty demands it, but because we are confident that God's hand is in control of the circumstances of each of our lives (Phil. 1:6), at the point of our obedience the sustaining grace of God comes all over us (1 Cor. 15:10) to perform whatever God has called us to do, even a life of drudgery. When his grace is upon us in such a sustaining way, the grace of God is related through us to the world around us.

> *If you keep faithfully at it year after year, you may never see the big and great things happen, but you will be able to look back and see that God gave the increase in his way and in his time, steadily, the way that has lasting results.*

REFLECTING THE GLORY OF GOD

The three years of the public ministry of Christ brought some big and great things, to the extent that after one of the miracles of Jesus, the Bible says, "And they were all amazed, and they glorified God and were filled with fear, saying, 'We have seen strange things today!'" (Luke 5:26). An emphasis, around which John centered his gospel account of the life of Christ, was his description of seven miracles Jesus performed prior to the Crucifixion and Resurrection. John referred to those miracles as "signs" (John 2:11) which proved that Jesus was the Messiah. As John was closing out his record of the life of Christ, he said, "And truly Jesus did many other signs in the presence of His disciples, which are not written in this book; . . . And there are also many other things that Jesus did, which if they were written one by one, I suppose that even the world itself could not contain the books that would be written" (John 20:30; 21:25). John's thoughts were speaking to the last three years of the earthly life of Jesus. Yet, only three verses in the Bible give us any insight as to the kind of life Jesus lived during twenty-seven of his first thirty years of life (Luke 2:40, 51-52).

Reference was made in the opening paragraph of this chapter how the Lord Jesus spent those "silent years" of his life. His life, up to the account about his trip to Jerusalem at the age of twelve, would have been like that of other children. He would have begun formal schooling during that period, but much of his time would have been spent at play with his brothers, sisters, and friends. After his return home from the Jerusalem temple experience at age twelve until the next recorded public event in his life, Jesus would have finished his formal education, spent less time at play, and learned a trade, which was carpentry (Mark 6:3), the trade of his earthly father, Joseph (Matt. 13:55). Through his teen years and early adulthood, the lifestyle of our Lord was characteristic of what this chapter is describing as divine drudgery.

Those years of Christ, prior to his public ministry, were not any less significant than those last three years of his earthly life, which changed the eternal course of mankind. Walter C. Smith captured the importance of those silent years of Jesus, as compared to the purpose of his public ministry, when he wrote the following:

> *Very dear the Cross of shame*
> *Where He took the sinner's blame,*
> *And the tomb wherein the Saviour lay,*
> *Until the third day came;*
> *But He bore the self-same load,*
> *And He went the same high road*
> *When the carpenter of Nazareth*
> *Made common things for God."*[20]

The way Jesus reflected the glory of God during the silent years of his life was significant, because had he not lived out the glory of God through a sinless life during those years, the Cross of Calvary would have been insignificant in its relevance to attaining our salvation.

Another purpose of divine drudgery is for us to *reflect the glory of God* we have seen in our "mountaintop" experiences down in the "valleys" of life, where most of our life is lived. The Jerusalem temple experience Jesus had at age twelve would have been a spiritual mountaintop experience for him in his early years. But part of the balance of life is that after those times of exaltation and exhilaration, they are usually followed by a

20. David Smith, *The Days of His Flesh* (Grand Rapids: Baker Book House, 1976), 14.

big let down of some kind. The wonder and glorious celebration of the birth of Christ covers thirty-nine verses in the second chapter of Luke, yet one verse summarizes the ordinary life he lived as a child (Luke 2:40). Thirty-nine prior verses describe his miraculous birth, the celebration that followed, and his temple dedication, then one verse portrays his childhood years: "And the child grew and became strong in spirit, filled with wisdom; and the grace of God was upon Him." Twelve more verses relate the incident in Jerusalem when Jesus was twelve years old, followed by two verses that summarize the next eighteen years: "Then He went down with them and came to Nazareth, and was subject to them, but His mother kept all these things in her heart. And Jesus increased in wisdom and stature, and in favor with God and men" (Luke 2:51-52).

The account of the life of our Lord goes from a glorious and marvelous Incarnation to thirty years we know little about. Even in those years we know very much about, which were unlike anything mankind has ever quite experienced before, Jesus and his disciples were not always on the mountaintop. One such example is found in the glorious experience of the Transfiguration (Matt. 17:1-13; Mark 9:1-13). Although Peter, James, and John were fearful at first, it was an awesome, unforgettable moment in their lives, as they shared that mountaintop experience with Jesus. Yet, when it was over, and they came down off the mountain, one of the first ones there to greet them was the devil (Matt. 17:14-21; Mark 9:14-29).

It is in the valley where we have to live out the glory of God.

From an intimate time of communion with his Father, Jesus came down from the mountaintop to the valley, where his first encounter was to rebuke the devil and to scold his disciples because they had not been able to deliver a boy from demon possession. From an experience of spiritual ecstasy to an encounter of harsh reality—that was typical of the life of Jesus and his disciples; from moments of signs and wonders to dealing with unbelief and spiritual immaturity.

The mountaintop is a wonderful place to be. We need those experiences, and we ought to cherish them. But it is in the valley where we have to live out the glory of God. We see his glory in wonderful ways on the mountaintop, and we just want to stay there. But it is not an experience from which God only means for us to benefit. We must take the effect of it down into the valleys of life and reflect his glory there. Down in the valley is where the meaning of what we have seen in our mountaintop experiences is explained and made real in the lives of others. Oswald Chambers brilliantly described why our lives count the most for the Lord in the valley:

> We have all had times on the mount, when we have seen things from God's standpoint and have wanted to stay there. The test of our spiritual life is the power to descend; if we have power to rise only, something is wrong. It is a great thing to be on the mount with God, but a man only gets there in order that afterwards he may get down among the devil-possessed and lift them up. We are not built for the mountains and the dawns and aesthetic affinities, those are for moments of inspiration, that is all. We are built for the valley, for the ordinary stuff we are in, and that is where we have to prove our mettle. Spiritual selfishness always wants repeated moments on the mount. We feel we could talk like angels and live like angels, if only we could stay on the mount. The times of exaltation are exceptional, they have their meaning in our life with God, but we must beware lest our spiritual selfishness wants to make them the only time.[21]

> . . . It is in the sphere of humiliation that we find our true worth to God, that is where our faithfulness is revealed. Most of us can do things if we are always at the heroic pitch because of the natural selfishness of our hearts, but God wants us at the drab commonplace pitch, where we live in the valley according to our personal relationship to Him. Peter thought it would be a fine thing for them to remain on the mount, but Jesus Christ took the disciples down from the mount into the valley, the place where the meaning of the vision is explained.

> . . . It takes the valley of humiliation to root the scepticism out of us. . . . When you were on the mount, you could believe anything, but what about the time when you were up against the facts in the valley?[22]

---

21. Chambers, *My Utmost for His Highest*, 203.
22. Ibid., 204.

It is not as easy to live for Christ in the valley as it is on the mountaintop. But the valley of drudgery has its benefits for you because it is where any skepticism or disbelief is rooted out of you. Up on the mountaintop it is not hard to be a believer, for it is where you see that all power in heaven and earth belong to Jesus. But your greatest worth to God is found in the valley. When you are rightly related to and faithfully following Jesus in the valley, his power flows through you there from the same source where you draw power on the mountaintop. Although it is not always manifested in miraculous ways, you see that the Bible is just as true, the Holy Spirit is just as real, you are just as saved, and Jesus is just as much your Lord and Savior in the valleys of life as on the mountaintops. Songwriter Brown Bannister expressed so well in his song, "Mountain Top," why we eventually need to come down off the spiritual mountaintops:

I'd love to live on a mountain top, fellowshipping with the Lord;

I'd love to stand on a mountain top 'cause I love to feel my spirit soar.

But I've got to come down from the mountain top to the people in the valley below,

or they'll never know that they can go to the mountain of the Lord.[23]

At my first pastorate, we lived a little over an hour's drive from the heart of the Great Smoky Mountains National Park, and just over a half hour drive from the perimeter of this beautiful mountain range. Several times a year, our family got to see the view from Newfound Gap, the highest observation point from which you can enjoy the view in your car. I have stood a few times upon the observation tower at Clingman's Dome, the highest elevation point in the Smokies. It was a beautiful, breath-taking view on the top. But I also

> *Although it is not always manifested in miraculous ways, you see that the Bible is just as true, the Holy Spirit is just as real, you are just as saved, and Jesus is just as much your Lord and Savior in the valleys of life as on the mountaintops.*

---

23. Brown Bannister, *Mountain Top*, (Bug and Bear Music, 1977).

enjoyed the view of the Smokies from ground level, particularly from the deck of our home, where, on a clear day, we could see the mountains thirty miles away. That is how I normally viewed the Smokies. It was a nice scene to look at, but it was even more meaningful because I knew what it looked like from the top.

Most of the people who live in that area see those mountains the most from the ground level. But there are plenty of people around them who have seen the view from the top and who encourage those who have not been there to go to the top. When visitors came to stay with us, we liked to take them to the mountains. Sometimes, time would not allow it, so we were only able to tell them what it was like. That is what God wants us to do spiritually in our lives. As some people will only see the mountains from ground level, from the valleys below, the only way they will know what it is like on the top is what they learn from those of us who have been to the top. We need to reflect the glory of God we have been exposed to as we live out our lives for the glory of God wherever we are, but especially in the valley of divine drudgery, where most of us will live out our lives.

CONCLUSION

In the introduction to this chapter, the statement was made that divine drudgery is the means by which the greatness, grace, and glory of God are most personally, impressively, and influentially manifested in the world today. It is the most personal way because those attributes are being lived out through you at the level of life where the vast majority of people live. Divine drudgery is not impressive in its effect as something big, great, and magnificent that grabs people's attention and causes them to marvel temporarily. It gives an impression that is made upon the hearts of people as they observe your consistent, ordinary lifestyle of dedication to the Lord, which naturally results in revealing God's greatness, relating his grace, and reflecting his glory at their level of understanding. But your ordinary life makes an extraordinary, lasting impression as your lifestyle witness takes hold of the hearts of people you are not even aware are watching you. You would probably be surprised to find out who some of your life observers are. But someday, you may, as the influence of your life leads them to eternal life through Christ. Praise the Lord for the ministries of the well-known preachers and evangelists of our day. But the greatest influence upon the lost people around you has not been the Billy Grahams, the Jerry Falwells, the Adrian Rogers, the John Hagees, or the Charles Stanleys. IT IS YOU.

Where will people be witnessed to the most for Christ? It is as we live out the glory of God by sharing with the world around us how we received our salvation through Jesus and by showing whose we are in our conduct and conversation. For most of us, it will be done in the realm of divine drudgery. One of the best illustrations of the profound influence of divine drudgery is seen in a plant known as the *century aloe*. This plant only blooms once every one hundred years. Not one of those years, though, prior to its blooming is any more important or any less significant than the rest. It takes every one of those ninety-nine years to get to the one hundredth year in which the century aloe blossoms. Then its glory is short lived, although the effect of its life continues on. The significance of this ongoing influence of the century aloe was the theme of one poet:

Have you heard the tale of the aloe plant,
Away in the sunny clime?
By humble growth of a hundred years
It reaches its blooming time;
And then a wondrous bud at its crown
Breaks into a thousand flowers;
This floral queen, in its blooming seen,
Is the pride of the tropical bowers,
But the plant to the flower is sacrifice,
For it blooms but once, and it dies.

Have you further heard of the aloe plant,
That grows in the sunny clime;
How every one of its thousand flowers,
As they drop in the blooming time,
Is an infant plant that fastens its roots
In the place where it falls on the ground,
And as fast as they drop from the dying stem,

Grow lively and lovely around?
By dying, it liveth a thousand-fold
In the young that spring from the death of the old.[24]

The years you serve in a place and position of service to our Lord may not result in your seeing outstanding visible accomplishments. The time of "blooming" may come during the tenure of one who replaces you in your area of service. But your having been faithful, year after year, will have helped to make possible their harvest. You may not live to see the evidence and effects of the new "plants" that will result from a spiritual harvest, but your life will have helped to produce them.

One more quote from Oswald Chambers is appropriate before closing this chapter because his few, but far reaching writings on divine drudgery have shown us the "high calling" of this divine discipline of God:

The tendency is to look for the marvellous in our experience; we mistake the sense of the heroic for being heroes. It is one thing to go through a crisis grandly, but another thing to go through every day glorifying God when there is no witness, no limelight, no one paying the remotest attention to us. If we do not want mediaeval haloes, we want something that will make people say—What a wonderful man of prayer he is! What a pious devoted woman she is! If you are rightly devoted to the Lord Jesus, you have reached the sublime height where no one ever thinks of noticing you, all that is noticed is that the power of God comes through you all the time.

Oh, I have had a wonderful call from God! It takes Almighty God Incarnate in us to do the meanest duty to the glory of God. It takes God's Spirit in us to make us so absolutely humanly His that we are utterly unnoticeable. The test of the life of a saint is not success, but faithfulness in human life as it actually is. We will set up success in Christian work as the aim; the aim is to manifest the glory of God in human life, to live the life hid with Christ in God in human

---

24. Mrs. Charles E. Cowman, ed., *Streams in the Desert*, vol. 1 (Grand Rapids: Zondervan, 1965), 238.

conditions. Our human relationships are the actual conditions in which the ideal life of God is to be exhibited.[25]

In a day where success, even in Christian circles, is measured by how much, how many, and how big, success, God's way, has more to do with character than statistics. *Success, God's way, is measured by what you are in comparison to what you should be in the will of God at this point in your life.*

> *Success, God's way, is measured by what you are in comparison to what you should be in the will of God at this point in your life.*

The true test to see how spiritually real you are is how faithful you are for Jesus in divine drudgery. It is the basic means by which God has chosen to manifest himself in the world today. It is how God has chosen for the vast majority of Christians to live their life. In the steadiness and consistency of drudgery, the greatness, grace, and glory of God are most personally, impressively, and influentially manifested in the world today. To some it is drudgery, but in its negative sense. To the saint, though, it is a divine discipline of God lived out to the glory of God in dedicated devotion.

---

25. Chambers, *My Utmost for His Highest*, 238.

12: THE PRODUCT OF DIVINE DISCIPLINE

"THE PEACEABLE FRUIT OF RIGHTEOUSNESS"

Thus says the LORD, your Redeemer, The Holy One of Israel: "I am the LORD your God, Who teaches you to profit, Who leads you by the way you should go. Oh, that you had heeded My commandments! Then your peace would have been like a river, And your righteousness like the waves of the sea." (Isa. 48:17-18)

In this scripture passage, God was speaking to a disobedient and rebellious people of long ago. One of the blessings that would have resulted from their heeding his commandments was that they would have had *peace like a river.* There is just something peaceful about a river. Some of the most picturesque scenes that come to my mind are rivers that I have viewed—from a bridge, while looking down into a valley, from the banks of a river, from a jet or airplane, or while riding in a boat on a river. The picture of peace in Isaiah 48:18, though, is centered more on the supply of a river than it is on the setting. The kind of river God was talking about was one that was abounding, everflowing, and sometimes, overflowing. Such depth of peace is what God wants to bring into our lives. But those disobedient and rebellious people of long ago were denied such peace because they did not heed the commandments of God.

Peace like a River

A product of divine discipline is peace, the kind of peace that is abounding, everflowing, and overflowing, no matter what your circumstances may be. But it can only come about in your life when you allow divine discipline to train you. That is dependent upon your obedience and cooperation. In Isaiah 48:17, God says, "I am the Lord Your God, Who teaches you to profit, Who leads you by the way you should go." Those words are just as relevant and applicable today as when they were first spoken. Whatever God does in our lives is for our profit. Chapter one dealt with the subject that divine discipline is "for our profit" (Heb. 12:10). When God does something for our profit, it is for our best. But we sometimes seem to think that we know a better way to go which is more profitable for us than God's way. Those to whom God originally spoke in Isaiah 48 chose to go their own way, and they missed the blessing of peace like a river.

Divine discipline produces the peaceable fruit of righteousness in those who have been trained by it (Heb. 12:11). It is a "peace like a river" fruit of righteousness. In the spiritual realm, peace and righteousness go together. In Isaiah 48:18, God not only tells us that obeying him will bring peace like a river, but it will produce "righteousness like the waves of the sea." There will be no peace without righteousness. Two qualities of peace are evident in the lives of those who have been trained by divine discipline.

The fruit of righteousness that is peaceable like a river is attained through divine discipline. The Greek word translated, "peaceable" (*eirenikon*), in Hebrews 12:11 has its source in its noun form, "peace" (*eirene*). In this verse, it is used as an adjective modifying the word, "fruit." The "peaceable fruit" produced by divine discipline is "righteousness." The literal sense of the word *peace* means a state of national tranquility free from the rage and havoc of war. The idea of that definition of peace is expressed in the word *freedom*. Peace also expresses the state of harmony between individuals. The word *fellowship* sums up the thought of that definition of peace. The result of peace in its literal sense, whether on a national level or personal level, is safety, security, serenity, and stability as a result of the absence or end of strife.

In its spiritual sense, peace is *the tranquil state brought about by the grace of God, wherein the despair and distress caused by the effects of sin are removed through one's accepting and receiving God's free gift of salvation.* It is brought about by God's mercy through which he has granted us deliverance and freedom from the penalty of sin by Christ's sacrificial death on the cross.

All Christians have peace with God through believing in and accepting Jesus Christ as Lord and Savior (Rom. 5:1). But all Christians do not have the peace of God which surpasses all understanding (Phil. 4:7). To know the peace that passes all understanding requires trials and difficulties. But if you are exercised by the divine discipline to which you are exposed, a peace superior to normal comprehension is produced in your life.

In Philipppians 4:7, the Greek word *huperecho*, normally translated into English as "passes" or "surpasses," also means to be superior, to excel, or to rise above. This peace of God is a height reached in the Christian life that a world leaning on its own understanding does

> *To know the peace that passes all understanding requires trials and difficulties.*

not comprehend. Even Christians who have not attained this level of peace have a hard time understanding it. So often, when God is teaching us something or leading us to do something, particularly during trying circumstances, he directs us to respond contrarily to what would seem most logical to our human reasoning. In a world that puts self-made men on a pedestal who have reached material heights of success, people so often act embarrassed, uncomfortable, or they just ignore or tune out the person who credits his accomplishments to the presence and power of Christ's direction and control over his life. In a world that has a payback mentality when someone has wronged them, they just cannot understand a Corrie Ten Boome, who forgave and showed love to a converted German concentration camp guard who tortured her, her sister, and her fellow Jewish prisoners. When you have reached such a level of faith and forgiveness in your life, that is when divine discipline has exercised you and you have been trained by it. It produces a peace that even the "storms of life" cannot disrupt.

Matthew Henry spoke of this peace as "a greater good than can be sufficiently valued or duly expressed. It will keep us from sinning under our troubles and from sinking under them. It keeps us calm and sedate, without discomposure of passion and with inward satisfaction."[26] Divine discipline produces a calmness, a quietness, and a tranquility in your life. Knowing that God has seen you through all your past experiences and that you can trust him to see you through your future experiences, the result is that you can live in peace and joy today.

BEARING MUCH FRUIT

> *I am the true vine, and My Father is the vine-dresser. Every branch in Me that does not bear fruit He takes away; and every branch that bears fruit He prunes, that it may bear more fruit. . . . I am the vine, you are the branches. He who abides in Me, and I in him, bears much fruit; for without Me you can do nothing. . . . By this My Father is glorified, that you bear much fruit; so you will be My disciples. (John 15:1-2, 5, 8)*

From those words of Jesus, it is clear that we are not just to bear fruit in our Christian lives, but we are to *bear much fruit.* In that passage from the fifteenth chapter of John, we are given the degree of quality that a third product of divine discipline is meant to bring into our lives. This product of divine discipline is found in the second word of the phrase, "peaceable fruit of righteousness" (Heb. 12:11). The Greek word, *karpon,* literally means, "fruit." In its literal use in the Bible, it is used to describe a crop that bears a fruit of some kind, such as grapes. But the word *fruit* is often used figuratively in the Bible to describe the result, outcome, or product that originates from something other than a literal plant. When the word *fruit* is used figuratively, in a positive sense, it means, "advantage, gain, or profit." In Hebrews 12:11, this word is used positively to express the product of divine discipline as the gaining of the peaceable virtue of righteousness in one's life.

---

26. Matthew Henry, *A Commentary on the Whole Bible,* vol. 6 (Old Tappan, N.J.: Fleming H. Revell, n.d.), 745.

The word *fruitfulness* would best describe the quality of this product of divine discipline, for the result is a life that bears much fruit. The productivity continues year after year. Although only one specific kind of fruit, "righteousness," is mentioned in Hebrews 12:11 as a product of divine discipline, other passages of scripture bear witness that there are other kinds of fruit produced by our being exercised by God's divine discipline.

The first step necessary to bear fruit upward is that you must take root downward. There will be no vine with fruit bearing branches until there has been the *planting* of the seed from which the vine will grow. To bear much fruit spiritually, one must first be in Christ. But once you are in Christ, by having placed your faith, belief, and trust in Jesus as Lord and Savior, you are planted because you are connected to the Vine (Jesus). Jesus said, "Most assuredly, I say to you, unless a grain of wheat falls into the ground and dies, it remains alone; but if it dies, it produces grain" (John 12:24). That analogy made by the Lord paints a verbal picture of the result of his dying on the cross of Calvary and his resurrection from the grave. We have eternal life and abundant life through Jesus. Part of our bearing much fruit is to lead others to eternal life and abundant life through Christ.

After planting and the upward fruit-bearing growth, there must be the *pruning* of the branches. One of two kinds of pruning is done to a possible fruit-bearing plant to get the best results: separation (taking away) or cutting back. The second kind of pruning, cutting back, gives an insight into the purpose of the divine discipline of God when we are living within his will and are already bearing fruit for him.

A branch of a grape vine can produce a large quantity of grapes. But often, that is to the detriment of the quality of the grapes. A large quantity of grapes may be produced, but they are not necessarily the best grapes. Some may even be defective or rotten. So the vinedresser will cut away from a branch that which causes disease or affects the branch in other ways from producing its best fruit. Even some of the good parts of a branch may be cut back so as to allow more energy to be diverted to what is not pruned away so that it can produce a stronger and healthier quality of fruit. The vinedresser may even cut whole bunches of grapes to yield a higher quality for the rest of the crop. The vinedresser does the *pruning for more power*. Everything is removed from a branch in the pruning process that will divert vital power from producing the very best fruit. This actually results in the bearing of more fruit because it is lasting, usable fruit. The pruning process produces a healthier, stronger plant that will continue to bear more fruit over a period of time than it would without the pruning. It will also be a higher quality fruit.

An almost daily prayer of mine is that I will bear more fruit for the Lord Jesus. In praying such a prayer, I must be willing to accept the pruning that God feels is necessary in my life to make me spiritually stronger and healthier in order to bear more fruit. I try to pray daily that God will take everything out of my life that is not like Jesus. I do not want there to be anything in my life except that which will glorify and magnify Christ. So I ask the Lord to shake those things in me that need to be shaken (pruned out) so that those things which are not to be shaken will remain and be dominant and prevalent in my life (Heb. 12:27). The Lord has done a lot of shaking in my life, and he is continuing to do so.

Sometimes, this pruning process—his divine discipline—hurts, especially when I see things removed from life that I am embarrassed or sorry about because they were even a part of my life. Some of the things God has had to shake out of my life were things I was not really aware of as being a hindrance in my life because I did not know they were even there. I refer to such hindrances as "blind spots," which are faults or weaknesses in one's life. "Blind spots" are normally evident to others but not to the one with the "blind spots." Through the pruning process, "blind spots" become known to you. You are thankful to get them removed from your life.

Productivity is the result of planting properly, at the right place and time, and of precise, proficient pruning of the branches, on the most advantageous spots, at the proper time of cultivation of the plant. For example, the pruning of a grapevine results in an abundant produce of grapes that are of the highest quality. The key to the grapes being so rich in quality is in the pruning of the branches. This produces a grape that is high in quality because pruning makes for a healthier and stronger plant. A healthier and stronger vine will continue to produce more and more grapes to the bearing of much fruit over an extended period of time— more so than if there had been no pruning.

The analogy of the grapevine that Jesus used, as recorded in John 15, describing our relationship to him and the Father, is a picture of divine discipline. As we represent the branches, we must be pruned—divinely disciplined—in order to bear more fruit and much fruit. Many Christians want to bear much fruit and pray that God will make them fruitful, but they are either ignorant, apathetic, or unaware of the pruning process. When it comes, they are not expecting it, and it totally blindsides them. They do not like the pruning process and may very well waver in their trust and commitment to God's perfect will for their life.

The pruning of God hurts, but it is helpful and needful, if you are going to bear much fruit. About the worst thing that could happen to you would be for God to leave you alone. But the person whom the Lord loves, he disciplines (prunes) as seems best to him, because it is for our profit and for our best (Heb. 12:6, 10). Because God loves us, he wants the best for us. Our getting the best comes in our being the best we can be. As God prunes us through his divine discipline, we must not waver, but we must allow it to exercise us to the highest quality.

> *The pruning of God hurts, but it is helpful and needful, if you are going to bear much fruit.*

Now no chastening seems to be joyful for the present, but painful; nevertheless, afterward it yields the peaceable fruit of righteousness to those who have been trained by it. (Heb. 12:11)

Rightly Related with God

Divine discipline is brought upon our lives to yield the "peaceable fruit of righteousness." Righteousness is the one main idea that God uses to describe the peaceable fruit produced in a life that has been trained by divine discipline.

Although the context of Hebrews 12:4-11 lists only "righteousness" as a fruit produced by divine discipline, the "fruit of the Spirit" passage in Galatians 5:22-23 adds other fruits that are to be evident in our lives: love, joy, peace, longsuffering, kindness, goodness, faithfulness,

189

gentleness, and self-control. Also, when we take into consideration that whenever the word *fruit* is used in the Bible to symbolically describe the effect of a godly quality in our lives, there are many other fruits that divine discipline can produce beyond those mentioned in Galatians 5:22 or Hebrews 12:11.

"Righteousness" does not appear as a "fruit of the Spirit" in Galatians 5:22-23, yet it is included along with some of those fruits in other Bible verses. For example, Paul said in Ephesians 5:9, "The fruit of the Spirit is in all goodness, righteousness, and truth." In 1 Timothy 6:11, Paul's challenge to Timothy was, "You, O man of God, flee these things and pursue righteousness, godliness, faith, love, patience, gentleness." He again urged Timothy to "pursue righteousness, faith, love, peace with those who call on the Lord out of a pure heart" (2 Tim. 2:22). In the verses that have just been mentioned, "godliness" and "truth" are also listed with some of the "fruits of the Spirit" as examples of fruit to be produced in our lives.

The characteristic that is mentioned more than any other as a fruit to be produced in our lives is righteousness. In Psalm 1, the righteous person is illustrated as a "tree planted by the rivers of water that brings forth its fruit in its season" (Psalms 1:3). In Psalms 92:14, the Bible says that the righteous "shall still bear fruit in old age." Proverbs 11:30 again uses a tree to illustrate a righteous person: "The fruit of the righteous is a tree of life, and he who wins souls is wise." Ephesians 5:9 has already been referred to, in which it is revealed that the "fruit of the Spirit is in all goodness, righteousness, and truth." Paul exhorted the Philippians to be "filled with fruits of righteousness which are by Jesus Christ, to the glory and praise of God" (Phil. 1:11). In James 3:18, the Bible says that "the fruit of righteousness is sown in peace by those who make peace."

What is the principle to be gleaned from the truth that righteousness is mentioned with the word *fruit* more than any other characteristic? If the fruit of righteousness is produced in a person's life, that person will manifest the fruit of the Spirit listed in Galatians 5:22-23 as well as the other fruits that are to be evident in one's life. Righteousness is a source of other fruits.

Righteousness is to fruit like the first two commandments of the Ten Commandments are to the other eight. Jesus was asked, "Teacher, which is the great commandment in the law? Jesus said to him, 'You shall love the LORD your God with all your heart, with all your soul, and with all your mind. This is the first and great commandment. And the second is like it: You shall love your neighbor as yourself. On these two commandments hang all the Law and the Prophets" (Matt. 22:36-40). Jesus revealed that in fulfilling the first two commandments, the result would be the fulfillment of all the other commandments. Even in making the first commandment your one aim in life, the result is obedience to the other nine. If you love the Lord your God with all your heart, soul, and mind, you will be faithful to obey and fulfill all that he has commanded you to do. Likewise, the attainment and fulfillment of righteousness in your life results in the bearing of all the other good fruits.

In the Bible, righteousness is a term used to describe the virtue, quality, or state of one who is as he ought to be. It is to keep the commands of God. Righteousness is also a distinct attribute of God that is used most often in describing his judgment and justice upon mankind. A few of the many verses in the Bible that exemplify this attribute of God are Genesis 7:1; 15:6; 1 Samuel 26:23; 2 Chronicles 6:23; Psalm 98:9; Jeremiah 33:15; Hosea 10:12; Romans 5:18; 2 Thessalonians 1:5-6; and 1 Pet. 3:12.

Jesus said to "seek first the kingdom of God and His righteousness" (Matt. 6:33). Our Lord said that if we would make that the chief aim of our life, then our basic needs would be met. God wants us to be righteous. The Bible tells us that it is a product of divine discipline. Of all the spiritual fruits to be attained in our lives, we should *seek it first*. It we are righteous, then the other spiritual fruits will naturally develop in our lives.

What is it to be righteous? To be righteous, one must take an initial step in order to become righteous. First, the process of righteousness begins in your life when you are saved. The Bible says, "For He made Him who knew no sin to be sin for us, that we might become the righteousness of God in Him" (2 Cor. 5:21). You become righteous before God through faith, belief, and trust in Jesus Christ. That is the point at which you receive the righteousness of God. Jesus has provided the way to the forgiveness of sins and the gift of eternal life in heaven (Rom. 6:23) by the blood he shed for us in dying for our sins (Rom. 5:8-9).

All that is involved in becoming righteous is revealed in Romans 3:21-26:

> *But now the righteousness of God apart from the law is revealed, being witnessed by the Law and the Prophets, even the righteousness of God, through faith in Jesus Christ, to all and on all who believe. For there is no difference; for all have sinned and fall short of the glory of God, being justified freely by His grace through the redemption that is in Christ Jesus, whom God set forth as a propitiation by His blood, through faith, to demonstrate His righteousness, because in His forbearance God had passed over the sins that were previously committed, to demonstrate at the present time His righteousness, that He might be just and the justifier of the one who has faith in Jesus.*

We are not only to *become* righteous, we are to *be* righteous after we have become the righteousness of God through our saving faith in Jesus. We are not only to be rightly related *to* God, but we are to be rightly related *with* God. Righteousness is to be further developed and maintained in our lives on this earth as evidence or our faith and belief in Christ as our Lord and Savior. Divine discipline is a means by which God develops and maintains a righteous lifestyle in us.

The great man of faith, George Muller, gave about as practical a description as I have found of what it is to be rightly related with God after one has become rightly related to God. Muller said, "This means to be more and more like God—to seek to be inwardly conformed to the mind of God."[27] Mr. Muller believed that if a person attended to those two things, then the promise of Matthew 6:33, "all these things shall be added unto you," would be fulfilled. God will provide food, clothing, and anything else you need in this present life if you will seek first his kingdom and his righteousness. Mr. Muller summarized how

> *We are not only to be rightly related to God, but we are to be rightly related with God.*

---

27. George Muller, *The Autobiography of George Muller*, ed. Diana L. Matisko (Springale, Pa: Whitaker House, 1984), 191.

a person lived the first half of Matthew 6:33, which is our half of the verse to fulfill:

> *Do you make it your primary business and your first great concern to seek the kingdom of God and His righteousness? Are the things of God, the honor of His name, the welfare of His Church, the conversion of sinners, and the profit of your own soul, your chief aim? Or does your business, your family, or your own temporal concerns primarily occupy your attention? Remember that the world will pass away, but the things of God will endure forever.*[28]

Mr. Muller said that he never knew a child of God who acted as has just been described for whom the Lord did not fulfill his promise, which is the second half of Matthew 6:33: "All these things shall be added unto you." Righteousness is conformity to all that God commands, appoints, and wills. That is how one is rightly related with God.

Righteousness is attained in your life when you get saved. It is developed and maintained in your life as you seek to do that which God has commanded and willed in his Word. There is one key quality to be lived out in your life that will result in your staying rightly related with God. That quality is *faithfulness*. Righteousness and faithfulness go together, particularly in their relationship to one another, as seen in their appearing side by side in the scriptures. David expressed that the Lord would "repay every man for his righteousness and his faithfulness" (1 Sam. 26:23). In Psalm 40:10, David said to God, "I have not hidden Your righteousness within my heart; I have declared Your faithfulness and Your salvation." In a prayer to the Lord, David prayed, "Hear my prayer, O LORD, give ear to my supplications! In Your faithfulness answer me, And in Your righteousness" (Ps. 143:1).

Isaiah prophesied about Christ: "Righteousness shall be the belt of His loins, and faithfulness the belt of His waist" (Isa. 11:5). The Bible refers to the risen, ascended, but returning Christ as being faithful, true, and righteous (Rev. 19:2, 11), confirming the prophecy of Isaiah. Those two references and the two from the book of Psalms are speaking to righteousness and faithfulness as being attributes of God and of Jesus Christ. But they are also qualities that are to be evident in our lives too.

---

28. Ibid.

Righteousness begins with faith and is lived out by faith through being *steadfastly faithful* to God's Word and his will. Romans 1:17 states that "the righteousness of God is revealed from faith to faith; as it is written, 'The just shall live by faith.'" The Amplified Bible translation of the same verse says, "For in the Gospel a righteousness which God ascribes is revealed, both springing from faith and leading to faith—disclosed through the way of faith that arouses more faith. As it is written, The man who through faith is just and upright shall live and shall live through faith." That verse quotes from Habakkuk 2:4. The Hebrew word translated as "just" in Habakkuk 2:4, and its Greek equivalent in Romans 1:17, can also be translated, "righteousness." Thus, righteousness has its source in faith. The evidence or sincerity of righteousness is proven by faithfulness—the living out of faith, which is best shown through works (James 2:18) that are exhibited in a daily lifestyle of obedience to God's Word and his will.

Divine discipline produces the quality of faithfulness in your life, if you allow God's discipline to spiritually exercise you. Faithfulness comes naturally for the righteous person who makes his chief aim in life to seek after God's righteousness.

> *Faithfulness comes naturally for the righteous person who makes his chief aim in life to seek after God's righteousness.*

When you have attained and you continue to maintain the peaceable fruit of righteousness in your life, you have reached a level of faith where you can face whatever God sends your way, without anxiety, without falling apart, without argument, but with an attitude of acceptance, confidence, cooperation, and thankfulness.

AN EXAMPLE OF THE PEACEABLE FRUIT OF RIGHTEOUSNESS

George Muller, whose description of righteousness was quoted earlier in this chapter, was a great example of one who knew the peaceable fruit of righteousness. His life was a beautiful picture of the working out of righteousness and faithfulness. His life of steadfast faith was one that never faltered and remained strong to the finish of his earthly life. He lived his life as a minister, yet he received no set salary from the churches or believers whom he served. His only support was from voluntary offerings and gifts from those he ministered to. He felt led to live his life upon the prayer of faith. In answer to those prayers, God provided funds as needed.

Established Upon Total Trust

When God led George Muller to establish homes for the care and education of orphans and poor children, Muller began the work in such a way so that financial aid and provision could not be expected from anyone except those whom God moved upon to give. Muller knew that God would impress upon the hearts of people to provide funds and other needs for the work. "In childlike simplicity, he looked to God, and all that he needed was furnished as punctually as if he were a millionaire drawing regularly on his bank account.[29] The ministries God led Mr. Muller to organize were *established upon total trust* in God for their financing and expansion.

George Muller began living by faith in God alone to provide for his financial needs and necessities in 1830. In November of 1935, he felt led to establish an orphan house. On April 2, 1836, to May 26, 1854, 558 orphans were under the care of Mr. Muller's orphanage. By December 9, 1859, there were three large orphan houses in the orphanage compound with seven hundred children in residence. During 1857–1858, the Scriptural Knowledge Institution for Home and Abroad, which Mr. Muller helped to establish in 1834, supported and assisted twenty-four schools, distributed four thousand Bibles, and provided financial aid and support for eighty-two missionaries. More than one million tracts and books were distributed. Thousands of lives were won to Christ through the various ministries that George Muller helped to establish.

For Muller, there were many times during the years when circumstances and situations looked bleak and hopeless. The amount of labor Mr. Muller performed, and the responsibilities which were his, were amazing by today's standards. The diverse variety of responsibilities would have been more than most others could bear. But George Muller always remained calm, peaceful, and prayerful because he knew the one

---

29. Ibid., 6.

whom he completely depended upon and relied upon in absolute trust was completely dependable and absolutely reliable. His greatest hope was that his record of God's faithfulness to him would encourage believers to develop faith like his.

God wants to provide today for more George Muller types, who will place their total trust in him to meet all the needs of their life. God will manifest his faithfulness and his righteousness to those who seek his righteousness and remain faithful to him, regardless of the circumstances and situations of life. George Muller remained faithful to God, even in the midst of great difficulties. George Muller attained such a strong, steady, steadfast faith because he had been exercised by divine discipline.

For example, he experienced *divine delay*. Upon the opening of a new orphan house, Mr. Muller recorded the following in his diary: "How precious this was to me after praying every day for seven years. This blessing did not come unexpectedly to me but had been looked for and had been expected in the full assurance of faith, in God's own time."[30] That is an excellent example of divine delay. Muller had sensed the Lord's leading to establish a new orphan house, but it took seven years for all the pieces to fit together to bring about the fulfillment of what God had spoken to him. He did not get dejected or depressed during the seven years of waiting. He did not falter in trusting God, but George Muller remained faithful in doing what a Christian should be about doing every day. Among the duties of the Christian life he remained faithful in doing, he prayed—every day for seven years regarding this desire God had given him—until he prayed it through to completion.

George Muller experienced *divine difficulty*. When a boiler leaked at one of the orphan houses, their hope was that it would last through the winter, although they suspected the boiler was nearly worn out. Muller stated, "For me to do nothing and say, 'I will trust in God,' would be careless presumption, not faith in God."[31] To know the condition of the boiler and the extent of repairs needed would require taking the brickwork down that surrounded the boiler. This could have taken days, and several hundred children would have been without heat. But Mr. Muller prayed and acted in faith. When the day for repairs was set, the first

30. Ibid., 227.
31. Ibid., 228.

really cold day of winter set in. He asked the Lord to change the north wind into a warmer south wind. He also prayed that God would give the workmen a desire to work. As the day of repairs began, the north wind turned into a south wind. The weather was such that no heat was needed. When the leak in the boiler was found, the workmen began repairing it, and they did not stop until the boiler was fixed. The workmen worked all night to complete the repair work. Within thirty hours, the work had been completed and the boiler was working properly.

Divine drudgery is an accurate description of the lifestyle of George Muller. Oh, there were many glorious, wonderful spiritual victories in his life, but much of his life between those spiritual highs was tedious, tiring, and commonplace by today's standards. But Mr. Muller let divine discipline exercise and train him so that Christ was glorified and that the name of Jesus was magnified above every name. The lofty purpose for which he began and proceeded in his various ministries was to show the world and the church that God hears and answers prayer. George Muller believed his purpose was better accomplished the larger his work became, provided he obtained the means through prayer and faith. He wanted to show by the example of his own life that God does not forsake those who rely on him, even in hard times.

> *The more he was disciplined by God, the stronger he became in his faith and trust in God.*

George Muller wanted to give visible proof of the unchangeable faithfulness of the Lord by simply taking God at his Word and relying upon it. The more he was disciplined by God, the stronger he became in his faith and trust in God. He remained strong to the finish of his earthly life. The result was that his hope of encouraging believers to develop faith like his own was fulfilled. The inspiring and challenging account of George Muller's life lives on a century later now, where the numbers reached with our modern day means of communication and publishing are far greater and more easily accessible than in his lifetime.

CONCLUSION

God wants to raise up a new generation of George Mullers. Divine discipline is a means by which he will train them to reach such high levels of faith as that of George Muller. Muller saw the visible results of his faithfulness within his lifetime, but the influence of his life has been far greater since then. The same could be true for your life.

Whatever may be your lot in life at this present time, let your life count for Christ. If you have strayed away from God's will for your life, or you are not sure what his will is for your life, then get rightly related with God. Confess known sins. Ask God to reveal sins in your life that you are not aware of. Then be obedient to God by being steadfastly faithful to follow and observe all the commandments and ordinances of the Lord. If you are not absolutely sure about the when and where of the will of God about a particular matter, then wait on God until it becomes clear. Do be faithful to do the normal duties and responsibilities that are part of the general will of God no matter where you are or what you may be doing vocationally. Then you can pray in faith, knowing that God will hear your prayers.

A prayer of David provides an example of a prayer you ought to pray concerning your life: "Show me Your ways, O LORD; teach me Your paths. Lead me in Your truth and teach me, for You are the God of my salvation; on You I wait all the day" (Ps. 25:4-5). Be about the work of the Lord where you are, as long as you are in a position in which you can ask God's blessings, and it is a position in which you can maintain a good conscience before God. If God wants to move you somewhere else to do his work, let him be the one to do it. He will make the way clear for you if and when he wants you to go somewhere else. As God disciplines you where you are, listen and look for what he wants to develop in your life. Keep in mind that it is not only for your good, but it is also for the good of others who will benefit from what God does in you. And always, through all of God's divine discipline, "my beloved brethren, be steadfast, immovable, always abounding in the work of the Lord, knowing that your labor is not in vain in the Lord" (1 Cor. 15:58).